Maharaja

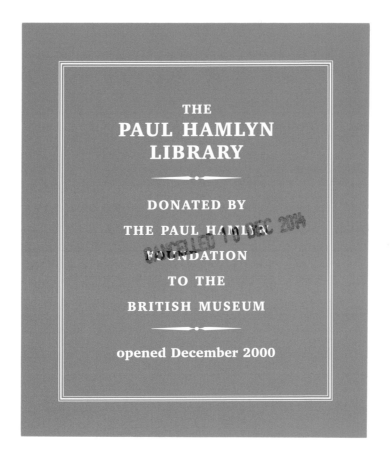

Maharaja

The Spectacular Heritage
of Princely India

Andrew Robinson

Photographs by **Sumio Uchiyama**

Frontispiece One of several ornamental gateways in the main courtyard
of the City Palace at Jaipur, built by the remarkable Maharaja Jai Singh II
beginning in 1728.

Title-page vignette One of the rulers of Jodhpur, the capital of the desert
region of Marwar, whose ancestral line dates back to at least the twelfth
century AD.

First published in the United Kingdom in 1988 by Thames & Hudson Ltd,
181A High Holborn, London WC1V 7QX

thamesandhudson.com

First paperback edition 2009

Photographs © 1988 Q Photo International Inc.
Text © 1988 Thames & Hudson Ltd, London

British Library Cataloguing-in-Publication Data
A catalogue record for this book is available from the British Library

ISBN 978-0-500-28822-1

Printed and bound in China by C&C Offset Printing Co. Ltd.

CONTENTS

THE PICTURESQUENESS OF ANCIENT AND NOBLE RACES

Raval Raghavendra Singh of Samod (*far left*) and Maharaj Kumar Ranvijay Singh of Jodhpur appear at a balcony in the palace at Samod. *Above* The immediate family of the Maharaja of Dhrangadhara.

'Amid the levelling tendencies of the age and the inevitable monotony of government conducted upon scientific lines,' said Lord Curzon, Viceroy of India, in 1902, 'the Princes keep alive the traditions and customs, they sustain the virility, and they save from extinction the picturesqueness of ancient and noble races. They have that indefinable quality, endearing them to the people, that arises from their being born of the soil.' Mahatma Gandhi, the son of a *Dewan* (Prime Minister) to a minor prince of western India, saw them differently. 'The present princes are puppets, created or tolerated for the upkeep and prestige of the British power,' he said on the eve of Indian Independence in 1947. 'The unchecked power exercised by them over their people is probably the worst blot on the British Crown.'

Today, we can regard the Princes with more detachment than either Curzon or Gandhi, but with no less fascination. Their descendants, their bizarre and beautiful palaces and fortresses, and the feudal loyalties formed over the centuries, live on, even if their despotic powers and titles do not, and their erstwhile subjects have votes.

In their heyday, the ninety years or so from Queen Victoria's proclamation of 1858, making Britain the paramount power in India, until the end of the British Raj in 1947, the Princes became bywords for excess, and for lifetimes spent in reckless expenditure and extravagant splendour unparalleled – certainly in this century – for their scale and refined inventiveness. One married off his daughter to another Prince (as late as 1948) in a ceremony described in the *Guinness Book of World Records* as 'the most expensive wedding in the world'; another conducted the marriage of two dogs with glittering pomp and circumstance in the presence of 250 other dogs in jewelled brocade mounted on caparisoned elephants, who greeted the arrival of the bridegroom by train; another had twenty-seven different models of Rolls Royce; and a fourth chartered a brand-new P. and O. liner to take him to London for the coronation of King Edward VII (being an orthodox Hindu, he had Ganges water sent after him from India throughout the six months of his stay). They included, too, the Nizam of Hyderabad, probably 'the richest man in the world' if only his valuables could be estimated, and a legendary miser who wore the same fez for thirty-five years; when he ordered his pearls set out for counting and grading, they covered the entire roof of his not inconsiderable palace.

Wealth such as this, coupled to the power of an absolute ruler, was also used for the benefit of the ruler's state. Some of the more enlightened Princes became as famous for their buildings, gardens and engineering schemes, their scholarships, patronage of music, painting and dance, and other good works, as for the profligacy of their households. One dynasty, the Maharajas of Jaipur, even founded a whole city (in 1728) which remains famous today as 'the Pink City', with careful grid-planning, beautiful pink stone in its construction, and matching pink paint on surrounding buildings.

Jaipur was one of the bigger states of Princely India, which consisted, at Independence, of 565 states scattered across the entire subcontinent, comprising about two-fifths of its total area. Like the Moghuls before them, to whom many of the Princes once owed fealty, the British ruled the remaining three-fifths: the coasts, the rich territories like the Ganges valley and the plains of the far south – leaving the deserts, hills and uplands to the Princes. The largest state, that of Hyderabad and Berar, was roughly the size of the United Kingdom, with an annual state revenue (in the 1930s) of about 85 million rupees; the smallest covered less than a square mile of land and yielded a mere few hundred rupees.

The British organized them in a princely pecking order which was pedantically observed by both sides and among the Princes themselves, who remained notori-

ously divided right up to their abolition in 1971. At the top were 118 First Division States, followed by a Second Division of 117 States and then, at the bottom of the league, 327 hereditary landowners. Rulers in the first group enjoyed absolute authority within their boundaries, those in the second limited authority, while those in the third had no powers of criminal or civil jurisdiction.

The First Division States were further known as the Salute States. This distinguished them from the other two Divisions which were both Non-Salute States. Each of the First Division rulers had the right to a gun salute on specified occasions, and of course the number of such salutes was strictly graded, following the lead of the King-Emperor (a 101-gun salute) and the Viceroy (a 31-gun salute). The five grandest rulers, those of Baroda, Gwalior, Jammu and Kashmir, and Mysore, and the Nizam of Hyderabad and Berar, received the biggest number of guns: 21. A further six rulers got 19 guns. They were followed by thirteen 17-gun states, seventeen 15-gun, sixteen 13-gun, thirty-one 11-gun and thirty 9-gun states. Generally speaking, the title 'Maharaja' was given to those commanding 13 guns or more; the lower orders had to be content with 'Raja'.

The exact order caused much bickering and squabbling between Princes, some of whom regarded themselves as seriously 'under-gunned'. In the 1930s a six-year argument between the Maharajas of Bikaner and of

Patiala ended with victory for the former and a note on the fat file created at the Government of India's Political Department: 'The Viceroy is getting very tired of the petty difficulties that arise over precedence.'

No doubt this was a tiresome diversion of the Viceregal energies, but it was his predecessors who were responsible for setting up the hierarchy, largely in order to divert Princely energies into disputes harmless to the real interests of British rule in India. From the 1790s, up to the defeat of the Sikh power in 1849, the armies of the East India Company fought a series of wars and concluded a series of treaties that steadily deprived the native rulers of military power while allowing them, in many cases, to retain other powers. As the able and somewhat cynical Mountstuart Elphinstone put it in 1832 to the Committee of the House of Commons on Indian Affairs:

It appears to be our interest as well as our duty to use every means to preserve the allied Governments: it is also our interest to keep up the number of independent powers. Their territories afford a refuge to all those whose habits of war, intrigue, or depredation make them incapable of remaining quiet in ours; and the contrast of their government has a favourable effect on our subjects, who, while they feel the evils they are actually exposed to, are apt to forget the greater ones from which they have been delivered. If the existence of independent powers gives occasional employment to our armies, it is far from being a disadvantage.

The Maharaja of Mysore was the first of these 'independent powers' to be created by the British, following their crushing of Tipu Sultan in 1799. Though he was part of the Hindu dynasty that Tipu had overthrown earlier, he had little of Curzon's 'picturesqueness' in 1799, being in abject poverty at the time of his 'rescue'.

The Nizam of Hyderabad had a rather more inspiring origin. The first Nizam was a viceroy of the Moghul power in Delhi who was sent to take over the Deccan plateau in 1724. By the time he died in 1748 the Moghul power had ceased to exist (though the Nizam continued to acknowledge his nominal allegiance to the Moghul Emperor). Successive Nizams saw their dominions becoming further and further dependent on the British power, though war between the two was always avoided. For a long time the relationship was one between near-equals; a respect for the Nizam's position reflected in the title by which he alone among the Princes was addressed – His Exalted Highness.

Central India presented a wholly different problem to the forces of the Company. They spent the better part of twenty years, up to 1818, subduing the roaming generals of the Maratha ruler, the Peshwa, based in Poona. These

9

were Scindia of Gwalior, Holkar of Indore, and Gaekwad of Baroda, who had all risen from humble origins. 'We were shepherds', explains the present Maharaja of Indore (who happens to be married to an American from Dallas). 'Apparently young Malhar Rao Holkar was sleeping by his flock when he was seen with a cobra reared over his head, shielding his face from the sun.' Gaekwad is derived from two Sanskrit words: *gae* for 'cow' and *wad* for 'gate'. 'The story goes that my ancestor saved a herd of cows from a butcher by opening the portals of his village and allowing them to enter. The British thought this was a title and started calling my ancestors "the Gaekwars" – or even "Guickurs" of Baroda.' (For some reason they also used a final 'r' instead of a 'd'.)

But the most cohesive group of rulers sudued by the British, and in many ways the most impressive, who might reasonably lay claim to being the epitome of Indian Princeliness to the outside world, both then and now, were the Rajputs ruling the desert states south-west of Delhi: Bharatpur, Jaipur, Jodhpur, Udaipur, Bikaner and remote Jaiselmer, among the total of twenty states in the Rajputana Agency. Nowadays they form the Indian state of Rajasthan. 'I still prefer the four syllables [of Rajputana] to the three; they seem magically to evoke a faraway, fairy-tale land,' Satyajit Ray has written. '[Though] I've been to Rajasthan six times, proximity has done nothing to dispel the aura that the place once held for me. If anything, it has entrenched itself even more deeply in my imagination.'

In a subcontinent renowned for its extreme contrasts, it is Rajasthan that seems to embrace them most fiercely. It has the harshest temperature range, the least rainfall, the brightest colours in the drabbest surroundings, the most convoluted turbans and moustaches, the most forbidding and the most intricate fortresses and the most enchanting palaces, and, in its time, the most enlightened rulers and the most backward. It also boasts some of the most striking women in India – 'women stepping straight out of the miniatures, decked out in brilliant reds and greens and yellows, disporting themselves with a grace that would rouse a queen's envy', to quote Ray again. These women also once honoured the most demanding tradition of loyalty in the world: *sati*, the self-immolation of a widow on her husband's funeral pyre.

It should therefore be no surprise that this 'enchanted land' inspired one of the classics of British–Indian literature, *Annals and Antiquities of Rajasthan*, published between 1829 and 1832 and written by Lt. Col. James Tod, 'Late Political Agent to the western Rajput States'. His three volumes burst with documentation of the tiniest details of genealogy, customs and long-forgotten wars and treaties – all infused with a passionate dedication to the welfare of the area and its people, the Rajputs.

This emerges clearly in Tod's conclusion to the introduction to the second volume of the *Annals*, in which he 'adopts the peroration of the ingenuous, pious, and liberal Abul Fazl', the author of the seventeenth-century *Ain-i-Akbari*, a gazetteer, almanac, dictionary of science, book of rules and procedures and statistical digest of the empire of Akbar, the Great Moghul, who died in 1605:

Praise be unto God, that by the assistance of his Divine Grace, I have completed the History of the Rajputs. The account cost me a great deal of trouble in collection, and I found such difficulty in ascertaining dates, and in reconciling the contradictions in the several histories of the Princes of Rajputana, that I had nearly resolved to relinquish the task altogether: but who can resist the decrees of Fate? I trust that those who have been able to obtain better information, will not dwell upon my errors; but that upon the whole I may meet with approbation.

One of Akbar's chief concerns lay in how to harness Rajput energies to the Moghul cause without destroying the Empire. He succeeded, through a mixture of force, the incorporation of Rajput forces into his own, and marriage alliances, thus inducing the Rajputs 'to become at once the ornament and support of his throne', in Tod's words. In the 1580s he took as one of his wives Jodh Bai, the sister of the ruler of Jodhpur. She became a powerful influence at the Moghul court and, as a Hindu, even persuaded Akbar to give up certain Muslim customs, such as 'beef, garlic, onions and the wearing of a beard', according to a disapproving Abul Fazl, who noted that 'the last three things are inconvenient in kissing'.

It may be surprising that the marriage took place at all when one considers the slaughter of Rajputs by Moghul armies earlier in Akbar's reign, which culminated in the famous sack of the fortress of the rulers of Mewar (Udaipur) at Chitor by Akbar in 1567. To avoid dishonour, nine thousand Rajput Princesses burnt themselves underground, and eight thousand warriors perished. This mass self-sacrifice, the third in Chitor's history, was known as *johar*. The young Prince Udai Singh, who survived it, abandoned Chitor for ever, and founded a new city at Udaipur, where a later ruler built the palace on a lake that is one of the most thrilling in the world. Unlike the other Rajput rulers, including those of Jodhpur, he and his descendants, known as the Maharanas of Udaipur, remained as aloof as possible from both the Moghul power in Agra and Delhi and, later, the British; they became the guardians of Rajput chastity.

Though Tod has an understandable tendency to explain away Rajput failings, or simply to overlook them, impetuousness, vengefulness and a degree of duplicity seem to have been as integral to the Rajput code of conduct as chivalry and extraordinary courage

13

and daring. Part of the Contents of one of Tod's chapters conveys the typical condition of Rajput life in the second half of the eighteenth century:

Raja Ajit – His assassination by his sons – The consequences of this deed the seeds of the Civil Wars of Marwar [Jodhpur] – Family of Ajit – Curious fact in the law of adoption amongst the Rathors – Ram Singh – His discourtesy towards his chiefs – Civil War – Defection of the Jarejas from Ram Singh – Battle between Ram Singh and Bakhta Singh – Defeat of the former, and the extirpation of the clan of the Mertias – The Mertia vassal of Mihtri – The field of battle described – Ram Singh invites the Mahrattas [Marathas] into his territory – Bakhta Singh becomes Raja of Marwar – His murder by the Prince of Jaipur – His son, Bijai Singh, succeeds – Jai Apa Sindhia and Ram Singh invade Marwar – They are opposed by Bijai Singh, who is defeated – He flies to Nagor, where he is invested – He cuts through the enemy's camp – Solicits succour at Bikaner and Jaipur – Treachery of the Raja of Jaipur – Defeated by the Chieftain of Rian – Assassination of Apa Sindhia.

And yet, such a catalogue of deceit and slaughter cannot be the whole story. Leaving aside the exquisite paintings, jewellery, silverwork, and carpets that were being produced at this time, and the incredible palaces within palaces that were being built (particularly at Jaipur), even the letters of the rulers are remarkable testimony to their powers of mind: 'they are sprinkled with classical allusions, and evince that knowledge of mankind which constant collision in society must produce,' says Tod.

He was in the vanguard of the British political officers who kept an eye on the Princes during the British period in India, usually under the title of Resident. He 'stood at the parting of the ways', observes Crooke, the slightly censorious editor of the 1920 edition of Tod's *magnum opus*, who was an Indian Civil Servant of a more settled age. Tod was besotted with the romance of the old Rajput life, but appointed to control it, in the name of good government. This he hoped the Rajputs would achieve for themselves, by his force of example without the Company resorting to arms; and he had too much respect for the Rajput rulers to want to reduce them to mere puppets.

Unfortunately Tod, and a handful of remarkable scholar-soldiers who administered northern India in the first half of the nineteenth century, gave way to British officers and civilians of a generally more rigid cast of mind, with some honourable exceptions. They were charged with the responsibility of giving effect to Queen Victoria's words in her 1858 Proclamation following the Mutiny, in which India's native rulers had mostly chosen to remain loyal to the British: 'We shall respect the rights, dignity, and honour of native princes as our own; and we desire that they, as well as our own subjects, should enjoy that prosperity, and that social advancement which can only be secured by internal peace and good government.' To which Lord Canning, India's first Viceroy, enthusiastically assented, enunciating the doctrine of paramountcy that the British were unceremoniously to repudiate in 1947: 'The Crown of England stands forth the unquestioned ruler and paramount power in all India and is for the first time brought face to face with its feudatories. There is a reality in the suzerainty of England which has never existed before and which is not only felt but eagerly acknowledged by the Chiefs.'

Having trumpeted aloud the ceremonial independence of the Princes in their internal affairs, the British soon set about interfering with them in practice in every possible way, with both good and bad results. One of the earliest, and most pathetic figures created by the new policy was that of Dhuleep Singh, Maharaja of the Punjab. Lord Dalhousie, the Governor General, had insisted he abdicate in 1849 after the second of two wars by the British against the Sikhs, which ended with the annexation of the Punjab. He also insisted that the Koh-i-Noor, the most famous diamond in the world, which came into the possession of Maharaja Ranjit Singh of the Punjab in 1813, should be presented to Queen Victoria. Both it and Dhuleep Singh, now seventeen and a Christian convert, were separately conveyed to London. The diamond was considerably reduced in size by cutting (from 187 carats to 109 carats), and came to decorate the young Queen's bosom; while its erstwhile owner, whose good looks were those of the young Dorian Gray, was taken under her wing. One day she questioned Dhuleep Singh's British guardian as to whether the young man regretted the loss of the Koh-i-Noor, admitting that she felt 'a certain delicacy' about wearing it in his presence. She was assured that he did not; on the contrary, its recutting had greatly interested him. So she took the opportunity to slip it into his hand while he was sitting for a portrait at the Palace and asked him whether he would have recognized it. Walking to a window, he spent a quarter of an hour staring at the jewel without speaking. He then returned it to the Queen, and expressed his pleasure that he could place it in her hands. But in private he called her 'Mrs Fagin', and said that 'she's really a receiver of stolen property. She has no more right to the diamond than I have to Windsor Castle'! Which indeed she had not.

This was but the first of the clashes between the Queen and 'her' Maharaja. As he grew up, he was in an impossible position; the British were determined that he should not return to India and excite dissatisfaction among the Sikhs, despite the support he had given the ruling power (at a distance) during the 1857 Mutiny, for which he received the Star of India from Victoria herself.

Living in Europe, unable to get nearer to India than Aden, he set the style for Maharajas in Europe to come. In 1864, he married a German girl who had caught his eye as he distributed prizes at a school in Alexandria. They had a son, Victor, who became the Queen's godson. Later, he became infatuated with a blonde who had been a chambermaid in a hotel in Knightsbridge; he required her to telegraph him twice a day when he was in the country. He also had a French friend whose liaisons included the future French Prime Minister, Georges Clemenceau, and the Duc d'Aumale, all at the same time.

He became a country gentleman too, with an estate on the border of Norfolk and Suffolk, bought, and lavishly furnished, with a loan of nearly £140,000 from the Indian Government. It became one of the first buildings in England (after the Brighton Pavilion) to be built in the 'Indian style'. There he entertained royalty and became known as one of the best shots in England. He also supported the village church.

Having failed to get to India he wandered Europe instead, and fetched up in Russia, where he hoped the Tsar might restore him to his throne by sweeping over the Himalayas. The British were not amused. Dhuleep Singh's wife, the Maharani, died (apparently of embarrassment and sorrow), and he sought out his mentor, now the old Queen, who was vacationing at Grasse in the south of France. They spoke à deux and, as the Maharaja began to ask her forgiveness, he burst into tears. Victoria was moved and stroked his hand in hers until he became still. He was restored to her favour, but not to that of the public's, and died in a hotel in Paris at the age of 56. One of his last acts, after the Maharani's death, was to take an English wife.

The rulers that followed Dhuleep Singh in the next generation were exposed in their youth to the full fervour of Victorian rectitude; the result, in some cases, was a truly exceptional ruler who used his absolute authority (usually advised by a *Dewan* and others, often themselves very capable) to better his state in ways that neither the Raj nor Independent India could achieve.

Probably the most remarkable of them all was Sayaji Rao, the Gaekwad of Baroda, who was placed on the *gadi* (throne) of Baroda by the British in 1875 at the age of twelve. His predecessor, Mulhar Rao, had been deposed for misrule, involving unspeakable cruelty to his subjects, extortion on a wild scale, and an apparent attempt to poison Col. Phayre, the straight-laced Resident. Mulhar Rao was brought to trial. His defence counsel was one of the most formidable British barristers of his day, who succeeded in destroying the Government's case. Notwithstanding, the ruler was removed.

His successor, who had been selected by a complex process of consultation between the British, the ruling family and Brahmin family priests, was the son of a village headman distantly related to the ruling family. He could neither read nor write, so his first six years at the palace were devoted to education; apart from two hours' riding, an hour for other suitable games, and meals, he simply worked, acquiring a lifelong taste for it. He also mastered four languages: Marathi, the language of his Gaekwad forbears, Gujerati, the language of most people in Baroda, Urdu, and English.

As John Lord has put it, 'Sayaji Rao and his Maharani brought Baroda out of the Middle Ages.' She had come from a village too, but she wrote a book – *The Position of Women in Indian Life* – that a British Prime Minister, Ramsay MacDonald, greeted as 'an extraordinary revelation of the educated eastern mind'. Sayaji Rao even went so far as to introduce the concept of divorce in Baroda. The Maharani, teased by her daughter about this, would try to be dignified and huffy, but would end up shaking with laughter. A trifle surprisingly, she was also the finest shot of her sex in India, eager for tigers.

Sayaji Rao opened the first high school in Baroda in 1881 and made education compulsory and free for the first time in India. Baroda's library system reached every village – an extraordinary achievement for that time or even for today, with the University of Baroda one of the most respected in India – and a science institute, art school, museum and first-rate picture gallery were also established. As he aged, Sayaji Rao became more preoccupied with religion. At the second World Parliament of Religions in Chicago in 1933, where Swami Vivekananda had made his first electrifying appearance on the world stage in 1893, Sayaji Rao spoke at length, observing that 'God is at work. He is a democratic king and asks our help. He recognises no hierarchy but that of service. Democracy means also the emergence of the common man, the demand of the backward peoples for a place in the sun.' This feeling found practical expression in his support for B. R. Ambedkar, the leader of India's Untouchables (who was educated in the United States at the Gaekwad's expense), and for Mahatma Gandhi.

But he was not interested only in good works; there was fun in him too, and a certain *élan*, but no hint of the debauchery practised assiduously by earlier Gaekwads, and to some extent, by his playboy son. Though his majordomo and valet and the heads of his army, police force, hospitals and colleges were all English, his cook was French and a couple of chauffeurs were Italian, because their cars were. His table linen was from Belfast and his dinner services from Bond Street. Dinner might well be accompanied by music from a small string orchestra under the baton of a French bandmaster who had composed Baroda's national anthem. Then there were his parrots, the 'favourite entertainment' of his grand-daughter Gayatri Devi, now the Rajmata of Jaipur, as she recalls in her memoir *A Princess Remembers:*

They used to ride tiny silver bicycles, drive little silver cars, walk tightropes, and enact a variety of dramatic scenes. I remember one in particular, in which a parrot was run over by a car, examined by a parrot doctor, and finally carried off on a stretcher by parrot bearers. The grand climax of their performance was always a salute fired on a silver cannon. It made the most amazing noise for a miniature weapon, and the parrots were the only ones to remain unperturbed.

No wonder Sayaji Rao fell in love with the White Rabbit and Lewis Carroll's other creatures, and commissioned a Marathi translation of *Alice's Adventures in Wonderland*.

He also commissioned, and lived in until his death in 1939, one of the largest and most catholic palaces in India, the Laxmi Vilas. The architects were two Englishmen, but the style was far from being English. The palace is three times the size of Buckingham Palace, with its kitchen two miles from the dining room; at one time the Gaekwad used a scooter to speed from his bedroom to his meals. In its heyday, he employed around a thousand staff in it. The present Gaekwad makes do with 150, some of whom remember him as a boy.

He himself recalls that as a child he used to run through the corridors and talk to the servants about the Mahatma. 'For ten years I drank only goat's milk,' he says.

Most ruling princes of that time had other things on their mind than Gandhi and the nationalist movement. Though they sympathized with the concept of independence from the British, they generally thought of it as the independence of their individual states, rather than that of India as a whole. They did their best to ignore the sensational occasion in 1916, at the opening of the Benares Hindu University, when Gandhi had told them in assembled splendour that 'There is no salvation for India unless you strip yourselves of this jewellery and hold it in trust for your countrymen in India. I am sure it is not the desire of the King-Emperor or Lord Hardinge [the Viceroy] that in order to show the truest loyalty to our King-Emperor, it is necessary for us to ransack our jewellery boxes, and to appear bedecked from top to toe.'

Instead, as the political manoeuvring ground on, the majority of rulers went on a spending spree, in India and especially in the grand hotels and night-clubs, the gaming-tables and race-tracks of Britain and Europe. From the Edwardian period onwards, but especially in the 1920s and 1930s, they became established as exotic blooms in the hot-house social life of the European rich – wining, dining, gambling and womanizing, buying up whole departments of the most fashionable stores as presents and furnishings for their palaces (some of which remained in unopened boxes, at Independence), and making their distinctive mark in cricket and polo, and in pig-sticking, tiger-hunting and shikar of all sorts in India, where they laid on elaborate programmes of slaughter for the Viceroys and senior British officials.

There is no doubt that the attitude of the British Government to the Princes in 1947, and especially that of Lord Mountbatten, India's last Viceroy (who was, after all, a Prince himself), came as a shock to most of them. 'It was like the French Revolution,' comments James Ivory, 'except that none of them went to the guillotine; they merely became private citizens.' Having loyally supported the Allied cause in both World Wars, they expected the British to ensure them a role as rulers before they left India. They did not take seriously the plea that Gandhi had made in 1942, just before he was arrested: 'I am a well wisher of the princes. . . . I would ask them in all humility to enjoy through renunciation.'

Their moment of truth arrived on 25 July 1947, when Mountbatten, resplendent in his white Admiral's uniform, addressed the Chamber of Princes and advised them all to sign Instruments of Accession either to India or Pakistan. There were three weeks to go till Independence, on 15 August. The Maharaja of Bikaner, one of the most enlightened states, was the first to sign, on 7 August, because, according to his son Dr Karni Singh, the present Maharaja, 'he had put his faith in Mountbatten and in the leaders of free India'. The young Maharaja of Bharatpur had to request Mountbatten's formal permission to sign, since he was too young to exercise the prerogative. The Maharaja of Jodhpur pulled out a revolver and told the secretary of Sardar Patel, the Congress leader responsible for the Princes, that he would 'shoot him down like a dog if he betrayed the starving people of Jodhpur'. The Maharaja of Indore, having long procrastinated, finally sent his signed Instrument by ordinary post.

Only the Nizam of Hyderabad, the Maharaja of Jammu and Kashmir, and the Nawab of Junagadh, a small state in Gujerat near Pakistan, failed to sign before 15 August. The last of these Princes was quickly sorted out by the threat of force by India; the ruler fled to Pakistan and his state acceded to India. It took more than a threat, but no actual bloodshed, to bring the Nizam to his senses in September 1949; he had been seriously considering breaking free of both India and Pakistan, and apparently thought he could do as he liked.

Kashmir's ruler, Hari Singh, a Hindu Maharaja, governing a majority Muslim population, was trickiest in the long-term; the problem soon became entangled in international debate at the United Nations. After the Indian army had repelled a Pakistani invasion, Hari Singh was eventually persuaded by the Indian Government to step down as ruler in favour of his son Karan Singh, who was more acceptable to Kashmiri Muslims. His father did not abdicate, technically speaking, but continued to hold anguished dialogue with the representatives of a more egalitarian age.

Father and son, who has prospered as a politician in Independent India and was the only Prince to relinquish his Privy Purse voluntarily (during 1971), epitomize the tensions in modern India between feudal loyalties and democratic ideas. Despite his father's opposition, Karan Singh pinned his colours firmly to Nehru and the Congress, and yet, as he admits of his father's rule in his memoirs: 'His administration and system of justice is to this day accepted by impartial observers as having been much fairer than those of the post-1947 period. Corruption was far less, and severely punished whenever it came to light.' This observation has proved true of more former princely states than an ardent democrat like Nehru, or even a not so ardent one like Mrs Gandhi, would ever care to admit.

Politics has occupied a number of Princes and a few Princesses since 1947, mostly without much satisfaction. They have generally commanded massive electoral support from their former subjects. Hanwant Singh, the Maharaja of Jodhpur, was one of the first into the fray, in the elections of 1952. Karni Singh of Bikaner, Lakshman Singh of Dungarpur, Madhav Rao Scindia of Gwalior and his mother, and Fatehsinghrao of Baroda followed him. By 1971, there were 24 Princes sitting in the Lok Sabha (Lower House) of Parliament, the year Mrs Gandhi succeeded in abolishing the Privy Purses granted at Independence.

These amounted to about two million pounds at the time (out of a total budget of a thousand million), the Maharaja of Mysore heading the list with £115,000 a year. An effort was made by the Princes to prevent the inevitable, but they were as divided in their resistance to Mrs Gandhi as they had been in their quarrels over precedence before the British Viceroy. To quote the famous cricketer, the Nawab of Pataudi (a tiny state south-west of Delhi):

I found many of them having fights that they used to have two hundred years ago, one not talking to another because somebody's great-grandfather had done something to so and so's great-grandfather. It was mind-boggling in many ways to me, but it showed me that if they could not get together in 1970, there was no way they could have got together in 1947. There was even one Prince who stood up and said, 'I'm afraid this is the last meeting I'm going to attend because my Privy Purse is 192 rupees and I cannot afford the train fare.'

The most glamorous princely politician is undoubtedly Gayatri Devi, one of the world's great beauties, who in 1962 as Maharani of Jaipur won 175,000 votes over the runner-up, the Congress candidate. This means, as she likes to point out, that the Jaipur family now appears in the *Guinness Book of World Records* for two 'wildly disparate events' – the most expensive wedding in the world (in 1948) and the largest majority won by any candidate for any election in any democratic country in the world. It also meant that she earnt the resentment of Mrs Gandhi, which culminated in her imprisonment, along with the mother of the Maharaja of Gwalior, during the period of Emergency from 1975 to 1977.

Her election campaign was an extraordinary experience for her, 'a campaign of love' from the people of her state, some of whom walked as much as fifty miles to hear her speak and felt very disappointed at her deliberate lack of jewellery. She came to the conclusion that the clinch was her decision to stand for the Opposition to Congress; simple though the voters were, they knew she could only be doing this out of a sense of duty, not for personal gain. Her husband, Maharaja Jai Singh, who had deliberately refrained from active politics, was initially doubtful, but then lent his support to her campaign. On one memorable occasion, in front of a sea of Rajput faces, he told the crowd that his opponents were accusing him of putting up his wife and two sons for election. 'They say that if I had a hundred and seventy-six sons,' he continued, referring to the number of electoral seats in the Rajasthan Assembly, 'I would put them all up too. But they don't know, do they' – a disarming gesture of confidentiality here – 'that I have far more than one hundred and seventy-six sons?'

The 'enormous, swelling roar' that greeted this remark, while flowers were thrown by the crowd, finally convinced the Maharani that she would be elected.

Other former rulers, eschewing politics, have taken to diplomacy, the conservation of wildlife, and business. Some of their palaces make hotels with an unrivalled cachet; who would not rather stay in the genuine article than in some of the new five-star piles in Delhi and Bombay that masquerade as Maharaja's palaces? Two of the earliest to convert were the Lake Palace at Udaipur and the Ram Bagh at Jaipur; and the last real palace to be built, the Umaid Bhavan at Jodhpur, is also now a hotel, with the Maharaja and his family still in residence. The vast palaces at Baroda and Gwalior have so far avoided the change, and most of the smaller palaces are faced with serious difficulties. They may not be suitable as hotels, their owners cannot maintain them, and the Government does not want to – because of the cost. Many are simply decaying, offering a uniquely romantic spectacle to the persistent visitor in search of royal India – its legends and its ghosts.

These live on with special resonance in the folk theatre of Rajasthan. There they perform (sometimes all night) the play *Raja Bharthari*, about a king who ruled a minor principality in the golden age of the Emperor Vikramaditya. He is an ideal monarch with one fatal weakness: his all-consuming passion for his wife,

Pingali. She betrays his trust and gives a ring bearing the royal seal on it to her lover, who passes it to a favoured prostitute. It is recovered and returned to the king. Shattered, he abdicates the throne and does penance in the forest, where he meditates at the *asram* of a saint. Finally, he finds peace and becomes the preceptor of the *asram* when his guru passes away. In the meantime, Pingali realizes her error, and tries to prevent her husband from renouncing the world. But he is adamant. Resigned, she enters the *asram* as a servant.

The reaction of a typical peasant audience in Rajasthan to this story, recorded by Uma Anand in her book *Mansions of the Sun*, reveals the true attitude to kingship of both the rulers and the ruled in India. At the climactic moment in the play, when Bharthari learns of Pingali's betrayal, 'a half-uttered moan swept through the crowd like the sound of wind-whipped sand. They knew Bharthari's pain as their own and accepted as he did, the verdict. It was not in the circumstances – the discovery of treachery, nor in the actions of others – the frailty of women, that the fault lay, but in Bharthari's own fatal attachment to the object of desire. . . . In a flash the *maya*, illusion, had dissolved like a mirage in the desert, taking with it the love, wealth, fame, power that the king, falsely, had held to be real. They could appreciate his decision, which to them seemed completely logical. . . . A king's passionate love had been transmuted by the saint into compassion for all mankind.'

Though in some ways the traditions of today's Maharajas are dimmed in their lustre and reduced in their scale, and if some, like purdah and *sati*, have all but disappeared, it is unlikely that what remains will follow suit. India has always been a land of striking contrasts and disparities, and Indians remain as ambivalent about such aristocratic values and pleasures as the rest of the world, if not more so. Why else is the Father of Independent India Mahatma Gandhi, and the symbol of India's national airline, a Maharaja?

1
DURBAR
CEREMONIES FIT FOR A RULER

'Durbar' is a word of Persian origin imported into India by the Moghuls. It embraces the entire life of a ruler's court. The British Raj took it up in grand style at Delhi, the old Moghul capital, first in 1877, when Queen Victoria was proclaimed Queen-Empress of India (though she did not come in person), then in 1903 when King Edward VII was crowned King-Emperor (when his brother the Duke of Connaught stood in for him) and, finally, in 1911, when George V was crowned (and came in person – the only reigning British monarch to visit India before 1947).

On that occasion – film of which appeared at the beginning of each episode of the television series *The Jewel in the Crown* – the tentage spread over 25 square miles of the Delhi plain, comprising 233 separate camps, the King's camp alone occupying 85 acres. The Princes and their retinues made their state entries by elephant, of course, and went through the elaborate rituals which the British had meticulously copied from the Moghul power. The 1903 Durbar included 'the Parade of the Century', in James Ivory's words; 'The triumphal procession of the vassal lords of the East during the Roman Empire could not have appeared more splendid.'

These gorgeous spectacles were simply the grandest and most public of the thousands of occasions at which the Princes encountered the British Raj in their own states, a dramatization of their subordinate status on a stage of staggering proportions, in which the red carpet unrolled to cover a whole city, so to speak, rather than just the railway platform in the capital of the ruler's state.

The opportunities for accidents or bungling of protocol by either side were unending, and they form a long catalogue of hilarity today. At the time though, they must have been the cause of many red faces among the British; fortunately for most Princes, blushes do not show up so much on brown skin! Karan Singh of Kashmir recalls two incidents – during Lord Mountbatten's visit to his father Maharaja Hari Singh – that seem to sum up the permanent potential for embarrassment.

At a banquet in Mountbatten's honour, there was a bell under the table which the Maharaja was due to press at the end of dinner, so that the band would play 'God Save the King'. Mountbatten, who was sitting next to him, was so tall that his knee hit the bell by mistake and the band dutifully struck up. 'All of us struggled gamely to our feet roughly half-way through the chicken curry. My father was furious and went red in the face, but luckily there was no one he could blame. Mountbatten laughed uproariously when he discovered what had happened, and a fit of giggles had me almost rolling on the floor, despite my mother's glares from across the table.'

Later, the Maharaja introduced all his officials to the Viceroy at a garden party. They stood in line in a prearranged order. But as the Maharaja rattled off the introductions he suddenly realized he was introducing everyone by a false name; one of them must have stood in the wrong order. 'I can never decide whether he or the officials were more disconcerted, but Mountbatten didn't seem to notice anything was amiss or, if he did, was far too polite to give any indication.'

Karan Singh was sixteen when he saw all this. By that age most young Princes had received a basic training in protocol, both at home in their palaces, and probably at school too. As a somewhat *avant-garde* gesture to the uncertain future, which he may later have regretted, Hari Singh had sent his son, in 1942, to the Doon School in the Himalayan foothills (where many of India's Westernized elite have been educated, including Rajiv Gandhi). The usual school selected for a major Prince was Mayo College at Ajmer in the heart of Rajasthan. Named after a Viceroy, it was founded in 1875 and soon became the 'Eton of the East'. Some idea of its uniqueness, and indeed its lack of resemblance to Eton, then or now, can be imagined from the fact that the heir-apparent of Alwar arrived there in 1890, aged eight, on a caparisoned elephant with a procession of trumpeters, bearers, camels and aides on horseback. He had 500 servants, 12 elephants and 600 horses.

The young Princes settled down in houses, as at Eton or any other great public school in Britain, but not houses that their British counterparts would have recognized; each house was named for their State, and they and their retinues were its only occupants. Each was a mini-palace in itself with archways, gracious terraces and *porte-cochères* 'where the chauffeur could keep the Bentley and Silver Ghost pleasantly cool, a few pristine schoolbooks scattered on the cream upholstery,' as Ann Morrow cleverly puts it.

Lockwood Kipling, the Principal of the art school at Lahore and the father of Rudyard, designed the Mayo coat of arms with Rajput warriors in red, gold, white, green and blue, peacocks and swords. But the dominant atmosphere was not Rajput; it was British, of a mainly hearty Victorian public-school kind. Excellence in exam results was not then expected (unlike today at Mayo); superb riding, shooting and polo-playing definitely was. Gandhi was right, in 1933, when he told the young Princes at Rajkumar College in Kathiawar (the first of the Princes' Colleges to be established, in 1870): 'You are confined as it were to hot-houses and are taught to believe that you have been gifted with special divinity by God. . . .' He was also right, at least by his own lights, when he added that 'I, therefore, feel all your education will be in vain, if you do not learn the art of feeling one with the poorest in the land.'

Among the Rajput Princely families the attitudes cultivated at Mayo combined with older ones to create a crazy calendar of celebrations throughout the year. Gayatri Devi remembers her first Christmas at Jaipur after her marriage as a fully fledged Western Christmas, intended to please the English governesses and nurses, with a tree and presents, while outside the tropical sun blazed down. In the evening, Father Christmas arrived, 'amid howls of delight', riding a State elephant.

Her family also celebrated the Spring festival of *Holi*, as it does today along with the rest of India, by covering each other with red powder and squirting coloured water from syringes. There are miniature paintings from the eighteenth century showing similar scenes in Rajput states, and Tod gives a vivid description of *Holi* being played at Udaipur in the early 1800s:

The Rana joins the queens and their attendants in the palace, when all restraint is removed and mirth is unlimited. But the most brilliant sight is the playing of *Holi* on horseback, on the terrace in front of the palace. Each chief who chooses to join has a plentiful supply of missiles, formed of thin plates of mica or talc, enclosing this crimson powder, called *abira*, which with the most graceful and dextrous horsemanship they dart at each other, pursuing, caprioling, and jesting. . . . No alternative exists between keeping entirely aloof and mixing in the fray.

Another Rajput festival concerned opium, which was traditionally grown in large quantities in the valley around Udaipur. Throughout the desert region of Rajasthan today, a traditional ceremony of welcoming a guest consists of the host offering him a sip of opium water from his palm. The Jodhpur royal family have formalized this as the annual Akhatji Festival, where relatives and local notables sip opium water from the Maharaja's palm, while similar gatherings take place in the surrounding villages.

Tod thoroughly disapproved of opium, reckoning that it 'robbed the Rajput of half his virtues', but at the same time he fully understood its importance. '*Amal lar khana*, "to eat opium together", is stronger than any adjuration. . . . To judge by the wry faces. . . . none can like it, and to get rid of the nauseous taste, comfit-balls are handed round. It is curious to observe the animation it inspires; a Rajput is fit for nothing without his *amal*, and I have often dismissed their men of business to refresh their intellects by a dose, for when its effects are dissipating they become mere logs.'

The most significant and profligate of Rajput ceremonies – and this is true of all the Indian Princes – relate to the coronation of a ruler and to marriages. Jagat Singh II of Udaipur, who built the Lake Palace in the mid-eighteenth century, was said by Tod to have spent nearly an entire year's revenue of the State (at the height of its prosperity) on his coronation. Until the late 1920s, when the Chamber of Princes insisted that Privy Purses be fixed at a certain proportion of a State's annual revenue (about ten per cent), it was not unusual for a Prince to spend half the revenue on a marriage. Gayatri Devi recalls that at Jaipur in 1948, 'The book of instructions to our own staff and all the young nobles who were helping us was about two inches thick, detailing every party, festivity, ceremony, and entertainment and containing programmes for each group of guests and for their staffs. Even the menus for the servants and the vantage points assigned to them for watching the processions had been carefully worked out.' The bride's trousseau on that occasion may be left to the imagination; Gayatri Devi's own, eight years before, came from all the best shops in Europe, though it was nearly left behind at the Ritz in Paris.

Her marriage, as the third and most junior Rani of the dashing Maharaja of Jaipur, was one of the most romantic matches in Princely India, at least since the coming of the British. She was the daughter of an equally stunning beauty, Princess Indira of Baroda, and the grand-daughter of the remarkable Sayaji Rao. Her mother had been strong-willed enough to marry the Prince of her choice, the Maharaja of Cooch Behar, a lesser state in north Bengal, rather than the totally respectable, immensely wealthy and very conservative Maharaja of Gwalior, who had been selected by Sayaji Rao; without telling her parents, she had written to Gwalior saying that she did not wish to marry him, thereby causing an uproar. She was thus in a weak position to deny the demands of her own daughter, who had been in love with Jai (as he was known) since they first met and rode together in Jaipur when she was fourteen. She tried to ban the match, and when she failed, she made her daughter wait before committing herself, but then gave in gracefully.

The marriage of Karan Singh, Maharaja of Kashmir, who is also a Rajput like Jai Singh, could hardly have been more different. His father had betrothed him at an early age to the ruling family of Ratlam, apparently in a fit of pique, to spite the Jodhpur family. Just as suddenly, when Karan Singh was about eighteen, his father broke the engagement off and made plans for a new one with a twelve-year-old Nepalese Princess. This time, says Karan Singh, 'as a sign of the changing times' – Independence had just been declared and Kashmir was in turmoil – 'my parents wanted me to meet the Princess.' The two of them ate in silence while their parents, in fact mainly their mothers, talked incessantly. 'After the meal we got into the car and I said "yes". The Princess was, I learnt later, not even asked about her reactions.'

They married on 5 March 1950, in Rajput style, though not in Kashmir but in Bombay, where Hari Singh had settled after fleeing from Kashmir in August 1947. The bridegroom's procession from 19 Nepean Sea Road to the bride's house Kutch Castle, also on Nepean Sea Road, took half an hour. It consisted of Maharaja Hari Singh, wearing a fabulous emerald and diamond crown with matching sword along with all his medals, relatives including several former rulers in their brocade, all led by an army band which was followed by twenty-four servants each carrying a silver tray containing jewellery, clothes, dry fruit and sweets as presents to the bride. They were all on foot. Finally came the bride-groom, in a light pink shirt, tight pyjamas, another long brocade coat, a red turban and a set of diamond jewellery, sitting in a decorated open Packard car, in 'solitary grandeur'. It was the property of the Thakor Sahib of Dhrol, one of the fattest men in the world, which meant that Karan Singh, who was then recovering from some agonizing leg surgery, could sit in comfort. During the ceremony, he was fortunately able to use his sword as 'an effective walking stick'.

His wedding concluded much as a Western wedding might, with a party, bar the huge black goat which was lifted over the couple's heads to avert the evil eye, just before they joined a glittering gathering of guests at which champagne flowed like the stream of Paradise in the Red Fort at Delhi. But, as Karan Singh rather touchingly recalls, he had married a thirteen-year-old girl whom he had met for just half an hour. 'When we finally got up to our room it was about two in the morning. After we had taken off all our jewels and brocades we realised that we were, in fact, very young strangers. And thus it was that we became man and wife.'

When Gaj Singh II, the present Maharaja of Jodhpur, married in 1973, roughly a generation later, he was able to enjoy some of the advantages of both the love-match and the purely 'arranged' marriage. An old Etonian who had also been at Oxford, he had already had a number of girlfriends in Britain when his mother suggested some girls of her own. Like so many young Indian men, he rejected them all, preferring not to look at a girl 'as if she were a goat or a cow and not a human being'. In this unwilling spirit he agreed to meet Princess Hemlata of Poonch, a state now in Pakistan, at one of New Delhi's best-known hotels, an inferior version of his own palace, the Umaid Bhavan. They did not hit it off. The Princess passed a plate of biscuits to him and he said 'No thanks' without even looking up. She thought: 'How stand-offish, so aloof; I am definitely not going to marry that snobbish man.'

Some time later though, one of Hemlata's uncles tried again. He telephoned the Maharaja and appealed to him to rescue 'the poor innocent girl'. The Maharaja allowed himself to agree to meet her again, on condition that they could be alone together. So they met for the second time, in a small Indian Fiat, and sat in it for ages, 'talking it over logically'. They decided they would 'grow together and learn to love each other'. The marriage took place in February 1973, and they seem – like Karan Singh and his wife – to be very happy together.

Some aspects of the Rajput wedding ceremony have

changed with the times (not least the reduction in the crippling expense), but the essentials have not. The bridegroom is still *Kesaria*, the 'saffron-clad one' – saffron being the colour of joy and life-affirmation – and he still touches his sword to the ornamental *toran* (arch) that hangs above the doorway to the bride's house, evoking the ancient custom of marriage by capture. And the bride still wears *churra*, the red bangles that symbolize *suhag*, the auspicious state of married bliss, and has her hands and feet decorated with floral and trellis patterns of henna symbols, which are as suggestive to the Rajput mind as lace lingerie is to the Western.

As in traditional Hindu families all over India, the auspicious date of the wedding is fixed by a *lagan*, a saffron-stained letter sent by the bride's family, usually a fortnight before the event. Every day after that the bride and groom go through the *pithe*, or anointing cerem-ony, in their respective homes. In the case of the Rajputs, the *pithe* is only performed three days in advance. This, says Uma Anand, a contemporary expert on Rajput customs, is because a fortnight was considered too long to wait in the old days; the bridegroom might have been called away to war.

Another custom peculiar to the Rajputs is most intriguing, involving as it does the peacock, a bird that is intertwined in the lives of the Rajput rulers and their subjects in a multitude of startling and beautiful ways, particularly on the walls and gateways of their palaces.

On the first night spent in the bridegroom's home, women sing *moria* (peacock) outside the bridal chamber. The story is of a bride who goes to the village pond to bathe and finds a peacock displaying his tail and barring her path. She pleads with him to furl his feathers and let her by, but he refuses. Instead, he asks her to come away with him. Unable to resist his beauty, she runs away with the bird. Her young sister-in-law, who has witnessed the seduction, informs her brother that the bride has eloped! A hunt for the couple takes place. They are captured, the peacock is killed, and his body and the bride are carried home. The peacock is cooked and the girl is forced to eat his flesh as punishment. Although she submits to this, she soon rises to her husband's taunts in a dramatic manner. The husband is speaking:

'Cook that, my beauty, clean it well,
then you and I, we'll eat together.'
Served on silver vessels,
he and she ate together.
'You ran away, my queen, with him,
now you so lustily eat his flesh.'
In angry rage the lady rose,
she flung her bowl aside.
'Go, maid, to the bazaar straight ahead,
on my veil have embroidered a splendid peacock.
Go, maid, to the goldsmiths' street,
on my bangle have engraved a shining peacock.

Go, O maid, to the tattooer, and
on my eyes have marked my beautiful peacock.'

'What can be the reason for the singing of *moria* on the
bride's first night in her new home?' asks Uma Anand.
'Is it a warning to the young woman about the sacred
vow of marital fidelity she has undertaken, and the dark
consequences of succumbing to illicit rapture? . . . The
macabre motif of a loved one killed, cooked and fed to
the ignorant or knowing victim, is found in varying
contexts in the myths of many cultures. The women
who sing *moria* do so because "it is the custom". They are
so used to the words, that possibly their bitter meaning
or implication is lost on them. One can only hope that
the same holds true of the newly-wedded couple as they
hear the haunting melody of *moria* outside their bridal-
chamber.'

This conical headdress covered in such beneficent Hindu symbols as the swan,
and the attachments which look like pompoms, are all carved out of pith, the
material also used for the lining of the famous *sola topees* (pith helmets) worn
by the British in India. The occasion is the marriage of the sister of the
Maharawal of Jaiselmer.

Chandrika Kumari, daughter of Maharaj Sobag Singh, ascends the stairs of the Ajit Bhavan Palace in Jodhpur, during her wedding to Dr Adit Singh. As a Rajput bride, she may wear only the auspicious colours saffron, orange or red. She has garlands of marigolds and henna on her hands and feet, while her companions protect her from evil wherever she goes with a red shawl canopy. In this particular wedding the actual ceremony of marriage took place at about two o'clock in the morning; the precise time is determined by the priest consulting an almanac. The bride's veil, which is tied round her head, is lifted, and the bride and bridegroom ritually exchange their first glances.

The morning after the ceremony, the bride's parents wish their daughter happiness and good health before she leaves the palace. Her absent husband's orange shawl, which was ceremonially knotted to his bride's yellow shawl the previous night, is draped over her father to prevent it from lying on the floor.

Overleaf Some of the wedding gifts
are spread out in the courtyard of the
Ajit Bhavan Palace. They include saris
and other rich materials, jewellery and
delicacies. Dr Adit Singh, the bridegroom,
stands on a silver stool to receive
his bride, now unveiled as his wife.

The bride and her parents return to sit beside the ceremonial fire, around
which the couple have walked seven times. The fire is built upon an
octagonal shape with mystical significance; the priest sits to the left. Later, the
couple visit one of the decorated shrines of the Jaswant Thara to pay respects
quietly to the bride's ancestors.

The education of the Princes was always a confused mixture of British and Indian influences. Mayo College, at Ajmer in Rajasthan, is the most famous of the Indian public schools, and the best endowed, as its lecture-hall (*above left*) suggests. It was founded in 1875 exclusively for the sons of the nobility.

The annual graduation ceremony, seen here in December 1986, is a high
point in the Delhi social calendar; a boy's form determines the colour of the
turban he wears. The Maharaja of Jodhpur (*bottom left*) was sent not to Mayo
but to England – school at Eton, university at Oxford.

The Maharaja of Jodhpur, celebrating his birthday according to the traditional calendar, stands with his attendants and family on the steps of the Jaswant Thara (*left*), and prays at the tomb of one of his ancestors there (*below*). Raja Jaswant Singh was one of the great heroes of Marwar. He struggled for more than a quarter of a century – until his death in 1681 – to outmanoeuvre the tyrannical Moghul Emperor Aurangzeb. In 1659 he led 30,000 Rajputs into battle against the Emperor and almost half were slain, but when Jaswant Singh brought the survivors back to Jodhpur, the gates of the Fort were closed against him by his own Rani – his wife – who told him he must 'vanquish or die'. It took a week to persuade her to open them.

The Maharaja of Jodhpur continues his
birthday celebrations. In the distance,
the Meherangarh (the Fort of Jodhpur)
rises up sheer and forbidding. Its
columns and walls are covered with
a plaster of crushed cowrie shells
polished to look exactly like marble.

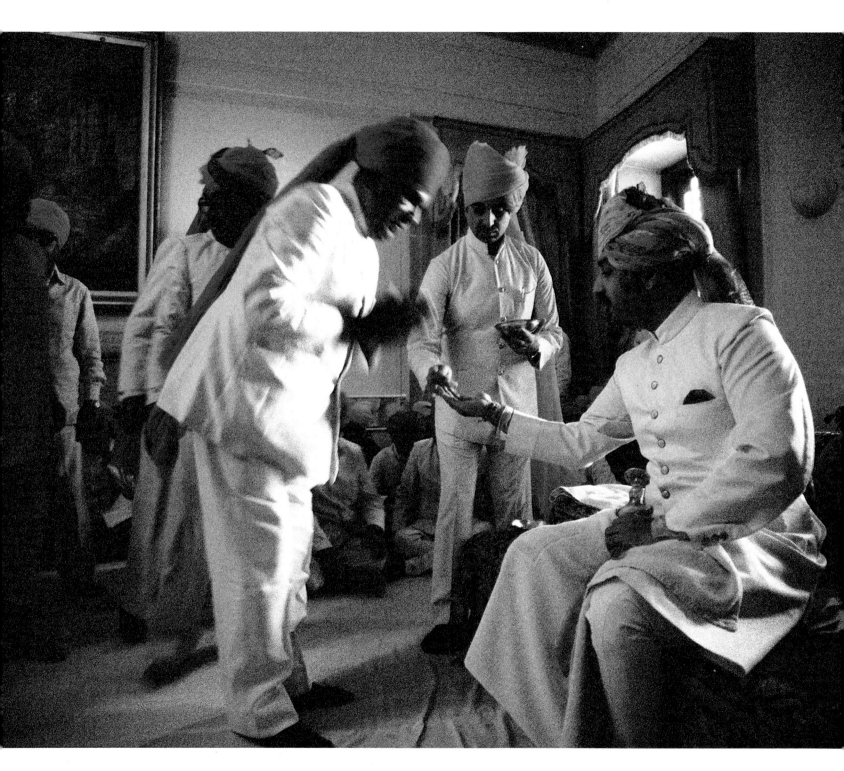

Among their vices, the Rajputs were known for their excessive use of opium. Today, opium-taking has been formalized. The Akhatji Festival takes place annually in June, the month of sandstorms. The Maharaja of Jodhpur is seen (*left*) with his relatives awaiting guests at the Umaid Bhavan Palace, and (*above*) offering some opium water to one of them in the palm of his hand.

Overleaf Men and women from a village near Jodhpur hold their own Akhatji Festival: one of a constant round of festivals that helps to break up the grind of life in a harsh desert land.

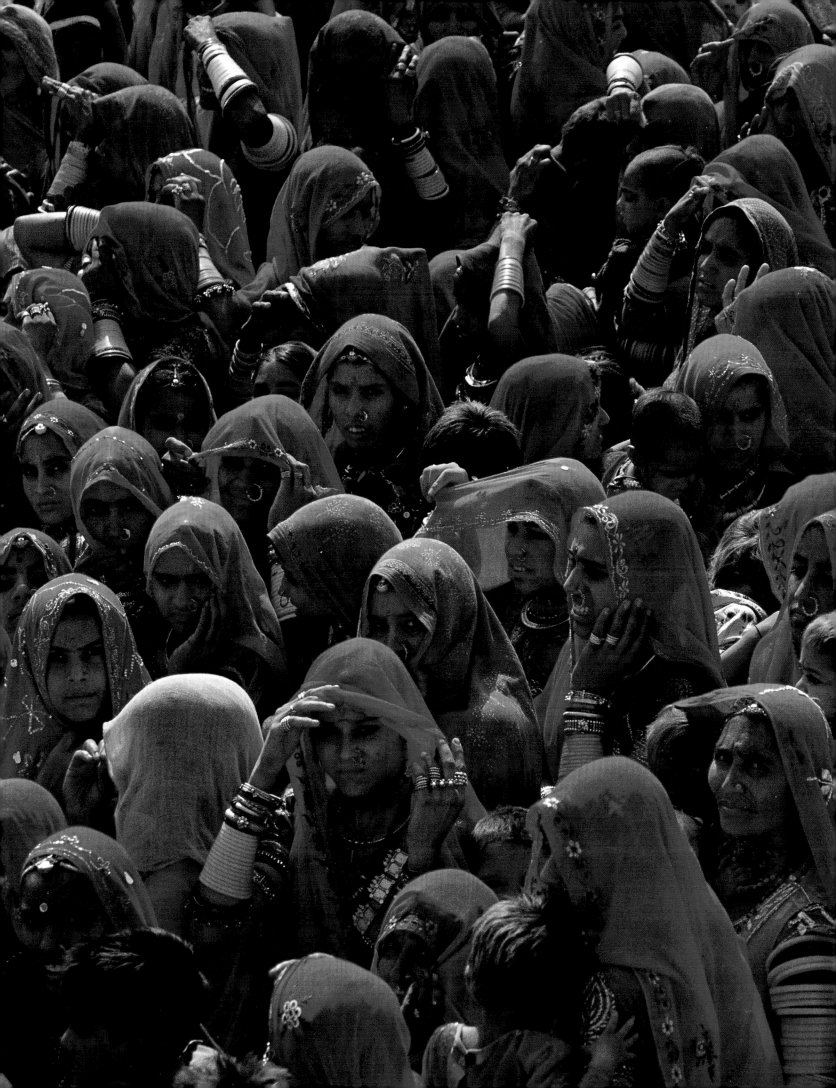

The Maharaja of Jodhpur celebrates
the nationwide spring festival of *Holi*
in the gardens of the Umaid Bhavan
Palace. Its roots are thought to lie in
an ancient and bloody fertility rite. In
one princely state, Bharatpur, *Holi*
lasted a whole week. At its conclusion
the Maharaja entered the city on
elephant-back, with a big water tanker
behind him, and hosed his people with
coloured water while they squirted
him back with hand-pumps.

The result of the Maharaja's efforts: his musicians – covered by him with red powder – wish him well.

Right The Maharaja, the Maharani and the Princess hug each other after playing *Holi*. Some years, the Maharaja is actually thrown into a tub of red water. There are Rajput miniature paintings of the eighteenth century showing that the royal households played *Holi* with no less zest in past times.

2
THE JEWELS IN THEIR CROWNS
HEIRS, HEIRS APPARENT
AND HEIRLOOMS

The Maharaja of Jodhpur and other
members of the royal family at
luncheon in one of the banqueting
rooms of the Umaid Bhavan Palace.

In *From Sea to Sea*, Kipling's remarkable collection of travel writings which includes his wanderings in Rajputana in late 1887, he observes that 'Jodhpur differs from other states of Rajputana in that its Royalty are peculiarly accessible to an enquiring public.' It was a perceptive remark, which is still true a hundred years later. The Jodhpur royal family have remained unusually open to Western influences and foreign visitors, while preserving their Rajput customs and heritage.

The present Maharaja's father, Hanwant Singh, was a flamboyant man, a pilot like his father (who was one of the earliest airborne Princes) and an enthusiastic magician: his English nanny gave him a box of tricks when he was seven, and he managed to become a member of the Magic Circle and perform before a large audience. He also secretly married his mistress in 1948, a nineteen-year-old nurse from Scotland called Sandra McBryde. She became a Hindu, wore jewelled saris and changed her name to Sundra Devi. After the Maharaja's death, she returned to Britain and took up nursing again.

He died tragically young, in a plane crash in 1952, having gone up solo to relax after a hard election campaign. The results were announced the next day; he had won 32 out of the 36 seats he had contested, a sure indication of the bond between ruler and ruled that led him to round off an election speech with the words: 'Enough of this nonsense! Now let's go to the temple and think about God.'

Gaj Singh is his only son. His mother thought him 'so blue and rather Chinese' at birth, 'what an ugly child'. He was four when he ascended the *gadi* of Jodhpur. His mother, and various other relatives, decided that if he stayed in India he would get spoiled by an English governess in the palace. So he was sent to a prep school in Britain, which he hated, and thence to Eton, which he enjoyed. 'It was a good period of my life, being abroad, because there I could be free. At the same time I used to come back every year, so I kept in touch with India as well. I did a switch in my mind on the plane. My sisters wanted to see me in my Etonian uniform, but as soon as the plane landed in Delhi, I would whisk off my jacket and be an Indian schoolboy again.' On his honeymoon he took his wife to Eton and then into the country with old schoolfriends for a 'green wellies' weekend.

Both there and at Oxford he was popular if a little withdrawn, no doubt partly because of the loss of his father at a young age. He was also brooding about his future. He felt that the mental switching between Britain and India was 'a good game while it lasted', but after Oxford it dawned on him that he had to learn how to retain the best of both lives and not become, so to speak, a latter-day Dhuleep Singh. Most people expected him to join the political world but he felt little urge to. Like Rajiv Gandhi, he preferred the certainties of a different world: in his case, the running of a palace and the consideration of how to convert it into a hotel.

He did, however, persuade his mother to stand for Parliament from Jodhpur. She won, but they supported four other candidates who lost. Though he has since served, with the Maharani, as India's High Commissioner in Trinidad, he has not been in active politics.

They have two children: a daughter, Shivranjani, born in 1974, who wears tracksuits and reads Enid Blyton, and Shivraj, a year or so younger. Like their parents, they are in demand by photographers: in 1986, for instance, they posed for Italian *Vogue*. They are sufficiently traditional to follow the custom of touching their grandmother's feet, a gesture which is in retreat all over India today, but not the customs concerning jewellery. Shivranjani likes to wear a gold ring in her nose, instead of the stud or clove which is usual for an unmarried girl: an urban fashion in India which should give its wearer a jolt, points out Uma Anand, 'were she to recall its original association with women slaves being literally "led by the nose"!'

Some of the family jewellery and ornaments worn by the married ladies of the Jodhpur household are very fine indeed, bringing to mind the lines of Sir John Betjeman's poem 'Summoned by Bells':

> Of shining showrooms full of secret drawers
> And Maharajahs' dressing cases.

Sir John's father used to make suites of ivory inlaid furniture for the Indian Princes in the 1920s. The jewellery kept in them was a mixture of traditional Indian settings and Western ones specially designed for them by the great jewellers of Paris, London and Amsterdam: Cartier, Boucheron, Garrard, Closter, and others.

From the time of the 1911 Delhi Durbar onwards, the jewellers' representatives would do the rounds of the Princes in the hope of carrying away lucrative commissions. They sometimes waited months to see the Maharaja; even on his third visit to Jodhpur, the man from Garrard, the British Crown jewellers, had to use all his powers of persuasion to make the Maharaja accept platinum mounts. 'He is afraid he will be seen as a silver prince and not as a gold one.'

The Maharaja need not have worried. The Maharaja of Baroda, a 21-gun Prince with one of the finest collections of jewels in India, had already commissioned Jacques Cartier to reset his entire collection in platinum. This included a coloured diamond necklace given by Napoleon III to the Empress Eugénie as a wedding present, a seven-stringed pearl necklace, the 70-carat Akbar Shah diamond (believed to have been one of the eyes of the fabulous Peacock Throne looted by the Persian Nadir Shah from Delhi in 1739), and the 262-carat Star of the South diamond (found by an African woman slave in the mines in Brazil in 1867). This giant stone was cut by Closter of Amsterdam to $128\frac{1}{2}$ carats. Maharaja Khande Rao paid £60,000 for it, settled it on a saddled and bridled giraffe, and took it through the streets of Baroda. He then placed it in a necklace with a lesser stone of only $76\frac{1}{2}$ carats, the English Dresden. By way of comparison, the blue Hope diamond weighs a mere $44\frac{1}{2}$ carats, the Koh-i-Noor, when cut, 109 carats, and the Regent diamond in the Louvre, $140\frac{1}{2}$ carats.

It was the sixth Nizam of Hyderabad, Mahbub Ali Pasha, who possessed not only the biggest diamond of them all, but also the most extensive and magnificent collection of jewellery of any Prince in India. The Jacob diamond, which weighs 162 carats, was purchased from a bizarre figure called Alexander Jacob, variously supposed to be a Jew, an Armenian, a Russian agent and a British agent, and credited with magical abilities. The Nizam paid him half the price he had asked, but when the Resident at Hyderabad came to hear of the payment, he took steps to prevent the second half being paid. While Jacob was ruined, the Nizam simply secreted the diamond in a drawer. The seventh Nizam eventually discovered it in the toe of one of his father's slippers. He mounted it on gold filigree and used it as a paperweight.

Mahbub Ali Pasha's pearl collection defied belief. There came a point at which he gave instructions for them all to be graded. Buckets and buckets of pearls were taken out of the treasury, washed in boric acid and then passed through grading machines of the kind used for grading gravel. They were then sorted and, finally, laid out to dry on the roof of the palace on huge sheets. They covered the entire roof.

But probably the best story about this jewel collection concerns the seventh Nizam's instructions to re-open the so-called English Palace, which had been closed since 1911, when his father died. When the official charged with this responsibility opened up the cupboards in the palace bedrooms he found expensive jewellery littered all over their floors. Mahbub Ali Pasha had kept pockets full of jewels everywhere he went, to give out as favours when the whim took him. At his death, the clothes had been left unexamined, had rotted, and their precious linings had dropped down below.

The Nizam also had large emeralds – the stone most closely associated with India (even though the subcontinent actually has no significant deposits) – but the ruler whose emerald collection was 'unequalled in the world, if not in quantity then certainly in quality', according to Jacques Cartier, was the Maharaja of Nawanagar. Cartier added to it a necklace of 17 rectangular emeralds, including a stone of 70 carats which came from the Turkish sultan, a close-fitting collar of 13 emeralds with two absolutely identical stones at the centre, two turban ornaments (one with a 56-, the other with a 39-carat emerald), and a two-string bead necklace in a rich green.

Cartier also filled 'casket after casket' of jewels for the giant Bhupinder Singh, the Maharaja of Patiala, to quote the house's official history. 'The designers had taken the traditional forms of Indian jewellery into account in the resettings, but the new pieces represented elegant reworkings inspired by contemporary art deco trends. It was surely the first time that Cartier had produced an example of the *nath*, a nose ring in diamond, ruby, emerald and sapphire, typical of south India. In addition there was ankle jewellery, armlets, a bracelet of nine planetary stones, and the exotic *hathpul*, a traditional piece of Rajasthani wedding jewellery worn on the back of the hand, linking bracelet and finger rings. No fewer than 223 pearls were drilled to create a single bracelet.'

The Rajput Maharanis who wore such ornaments were a formidable group. Until the late 1940s (and after, in some cases) they were in purdah, restricted to a life in the zenana; but some of them did manage to emerge on occasions, and there were exceptions like Gayatri Devi (who was not originally a Rajput) who combined public purdah in Jaipur with a considerable relaxation of it within the palace itself, and those legendary women whose 'influence on Rajput society is marked in every page of Hindu society', according to Tod, writing in 1832. 'What led to the wars of Rama? the rape of Sita. What rendered deadly the feuds of the Yadus? the insult to Draupadi. What made Prince Nala an exile from Narwar? his love for Damayanti. What made Raja Bharthari abandon the throne of Avanti? the loss of Pingali. What subjected the Hindu to the dominion of the Islamite? the rape of the Princesses of Kanauj.'

The generation of royal ladies who came to maturity around the time that the Princely States ceased to be, were divided in their feeling towards purdah. The Rajmata of Jodhpur, the present Maharaja's mother, ceased to observe purdah upon the sudden death of her husband, though unwillingly. Another Jodhpur Princess, the second wife of Maharaja Jai Singh of Jaipur, made it clear to his newly arrived third wife, Gayatri Devi, that she had no wish to 'come out'. And even the cosmopolitan Gayatri Devi herself, who had been everywhere and done everything by Jaipur purdah standards before she married Jai, could write in her memoirs that the first few bewildering months of her life at the City Palace 'showed me that it was possible to be lonely surrounded by people, yet happy when in the enveloping shroud of purdah life'. Not the least of its advantages, shared by her co-wife, was 'being able to go to the cinema in the palace in pyjamas and dressing-gown in the certainty that nobody would be able to see how we were dressed.'

The purdah method of medical diagnosis could also be turned to advantage, as the second wife explained. The (male) doctor would stand in the passage outside her rooms and obtain details of her symptoms – temperature, pulse and so on – from the maids. If the Maharani wanted to avoid a boring engagement she would simply dip her thermometer in hot water and have it sent to the doctor.

Udaipur, being the 'purest' of the Rajput states, had one of the strictest purdah regimes. The purdah cars in Jaipur in the 1940s had darkened glass in the windows; in Udaipur the royal ladies were carried around in boxes with heavy wooden shutters, as Gayatri Devi was discomfited to discover when she was invited there in 1943, along with the Jodhpur royal family, for a formal visit. She was looking forward to seeing the Lake Palace, but the boat she was put in was tightly veiled with curtains. She cautiously lifted a curtain to take a photograph. 'This rash act must have reached the ears of the Maharana, for later, on our departure, he pointedly presented me with an album of photographs.' She also had the *éclat*, standing among a group of at least fifty jostling purdah ladies, to fell a wild boar with her first shot, having failed to realize in the first place that she was expected to follow the lead of the Maharani of Jodhpur and her co-wife from Jaipur, and decline the offer. If she had missed, Jaipur's honour would have been badly tarnished.

Such a complex web of social attitudes perhaps helps to explain that most famous of Rajput customs, *sati*, the immolation of a wife on her husband's funeral pyre. The actual meaning of the word is 'pure'; it is believed that the wife not only attains redemption for herself, but, through her sacrifice, redeems the sins of her husband too. A woman does not therefore 'commit' *sati*, as one might commit suicide, but 'becomes' *sati*, that is 'she takes on a new, pure, radiant being', in Uma Anand's words. This, of course, has meaning only if she acts voluntarily, and not through any coercion.

In the annals of Marwar, 'the region of death', whose capital is Jodhpur, Tod was horrified to record that 'no less than sixty-four females accompanied the shade of Ajit [an eighteenth-century ruler] to the mansion of the sun. But this is twenty short of the number who became *sati* when Raja Budh Singh of Bundi was drowned!'

By the time Kipling reached Jodhpur in 1887, *sati* had officially been outlawed by the British for over half a century, but he reported, again with prescience, that 'in this land . . . men speak of *sati*, which is generally supposed to be out of date in a manner which makes it seem very near and vivid.' Perhaps he was also thinking of that cluster of grim-looking hand imprints at the gate of the Meherangarh, the Fort of Jodhpur, each one of which is a symbol of a *sati* and which are kept freshly anointed with red dye, even today.

In September 1987 an eighteen-year-old Rajput girl in a village near Jaipur became *sati*, apparently entirely by her own wish. Her act divided Indian opinion and led to a large pro-*sati* demonstration in the streets of Jaipur.

The last recorded instance of a royal *sati* took place in Jodhpur as recently as the late 1950s. She was Sugankunverba, the widow of Brigadier Jabbar Singh Sisodia of the Jodhpur Lancers, the grandson of Sir Pratap Singh of Jodhpur. Her story is told in Charles

Allen's and Sharada Dwivedi's *Lives of the Indian Princes* by her close friend Maharani Padmavati Gaekwad of Baroda, the only daughter of Maharaja Umaid Singh of Jodhpur. It is worth quoting in full since it is a moving statement of the presiding spirit of the ruling house of Jodhpur:

About a month before he died she stopped eating and drinking. She went about her household chores, looked after her husband and nursed him, but without letting on she got together all the things required for the last rites. I used to go to their house to cheer them up and one evening just a little before sundown as I drove into the compound, I heard this very deep chanting of *Ram-Ram* as if coming from a deep, echoing chasm. He had passed away two minutes earlier and she had already announced that she was going to commit *sati* when he was cremated at sunrise. While they attended to his body she went to her bathroom, had a bath and put on the brand-new clothes she had stored in her trunk. For *sati* we don't wear widow's clothes but wedding clothes, with the ivory bangles and everything. The colour she chose was a sort of light pink called *saptalu*, which none of the wives of the Sisodias can now wear because they now do puja to that colour. When she had dressed she sat with her husband's head on her lap all night. Twice his body perspired and twice she wiped it down

saying, 'Why are you impatient, I am coming with you. Be calm. The sun's first rays are still to come.' Morning came and her brother-in-law arrived, who was going to perform the last rites. When he doubted her intentions she got up and sat over the lamp which they kept burning near the dead body. She fanned the flames with the hem of her sari and sat there for five minutes until he said, 'I'm satisfied'. Now normally when a *sati* goes to the pyre she is accompanied by a procession, but the word had spread like wildfire through the whole city and people started gathering. So she said, 'We can't walk. Bring cars and a truck,' and in this way they avoided the police who were waiting at the entrance to the big burning ghat. She had sent for me, but I didn't get the message and got there late and by that time the flames had got too high for me to see her – but I heard her voice saying *Ram-Ram*, which never stopped for a second until she died. She is worshipped today not only by Rajputs but by everybody and so many *artis* [songs] and *bhajans* [hymns] have been composed about her, and her funeral pyre burnt for almost six months non-stop with all the coconuts that people kept putting on it. That was after they had picked out the remains and immersed them in the Ganges at Hardwar.

Earlier rulers of Jodhpur and their Ranis were burnt at Mandore outside Jodhpur. 'They seldom burnt alone,' says Tod, 'but were accompanied by all that made life agreeable or poisoned its enjoyment.' Elaborate cenotaphs roost like some species of prehistoric bird on the spots where the pyres once stood. Today, part-ruined, they inspire a kind of creepy awe. To Tod, gazing at them more than a century and a half ago, there came irresistibly to his mind some lines from his contemporary Byron:

There is a power
And magic in the ruined battlement,
For which the palace of the present hour
Must yield its pomp, and wait till ages are its
dower.

At the wedding of Chandrika Kumari, the married ladies of her family assist her to put on her jewellery and ornaments. The number of such helpers should always be uneven, usually five or seven. Apart from precious metals and jewels the bride wears only red for the ceremony itself.

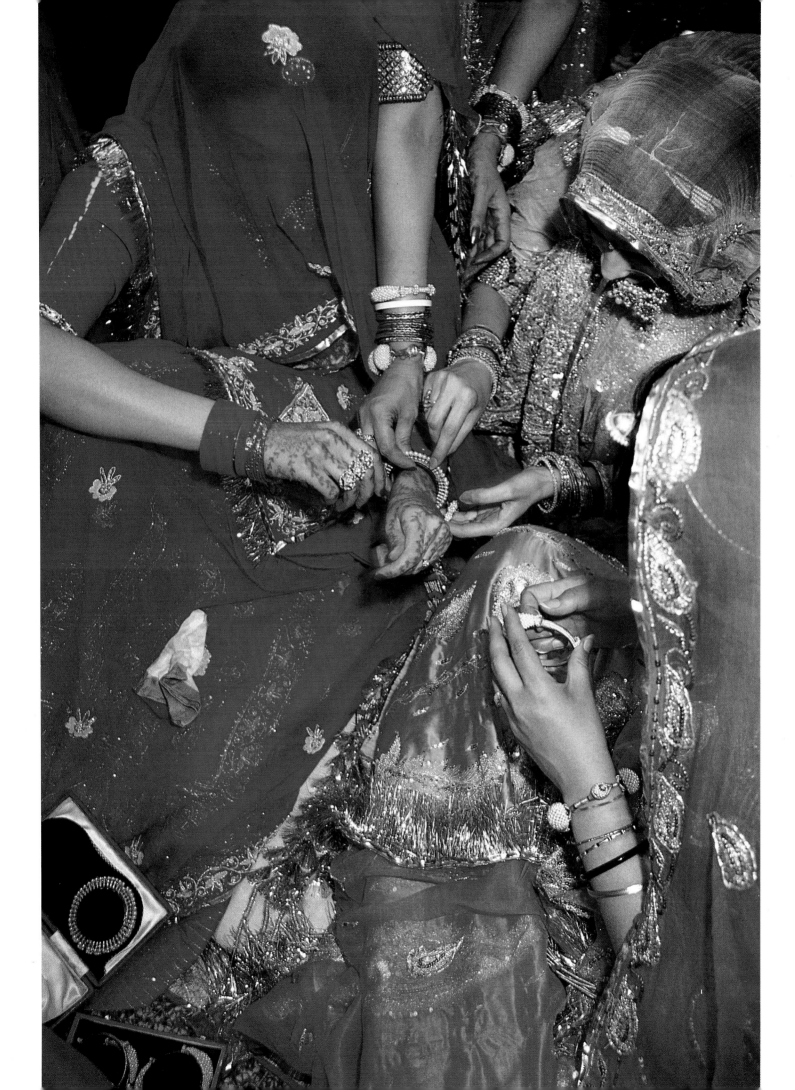

The Maharani of Jodhpur (*right*) and
Rani Usha Devi (*far right*) wear
necklaces that make it perfectly easy to
believe that an earlier eighteen-year-
old Maharani of Jodhpur had to be
supported by two attendants in order
to stand – her jewels were more than
her own weight. They included such
amusing trifles as eyebrows made out
of diamonds, now to be found in the
museum at the Fort. Male rulers were,
if anything, even more heavily
festooned.

'Diamonds', observed someone on the Prince of Wales's tour of India in 1875, 'seem as plentiful in India as blackberries in England.' India's Maharajas had some of the finest in the world too, including the Koh-i-Noor and the even bigger 162-carat Jacob Diamond, owned by the Nizam of Hyderabad. Rani Usha Devi shows off some of her own finery.

Overleaf Maharaj Swarup Singh (*left*) and Maharaj Dalip Singh (*right*) sport turbans with diamond settings of family portraits. Dalip Singh's depicts his father, Maharaja Umaid Singh of Jodhpur. In 1926, the representative from Garrard, the British Crown jewellers, had the greatest difficulty in cajoling the Maharaja to accept platinum mounts. 'He is afraid he will be seen as a silver prince not a gold one.'

For centuries, Jaiselmer, founded in 1156 out in the western reaches of the Thar Desert towards Baluchistan, was one of the remotest and most wonderful fortress cities in Rajasthan. Kipling, wandering India in the 1880s, did not manage to get there, but he observed that its family crest is blazoned with 'a naked left arm holding a broken spear, because, the legend goes, Jeysulmir was once galled by a horse with a magic spear. They tell the story today, but', he warned, 'it is a long one.' The Maharawal of Jaiselmer, Brajraj Singh (*second from right*), seen here with his brother Prithwiraj Singh (*far right*), succeeded in 1981 on the early death of his father, the son of the imposing Rajmata (*right*).

72

Overleaf The royal ladies of the house of Jaiselmer sit together at the wedding of the sister of the Maharawal. On the far left is another sister, and next to her is their mother, a lady of unusual spirit, now widowed.

The Maharaja of Jodhpur, Gaj Singh II, stands in the courtyard of the Moti Mahal (Pearl Palace) inside the Fort, with his son the Maharaj Kumar Shivraj Singh (born in 1975). His own father, Maharaja Hanwant Singh, a keen aviator, died in an air crash in 1952, when his son was only four years old.

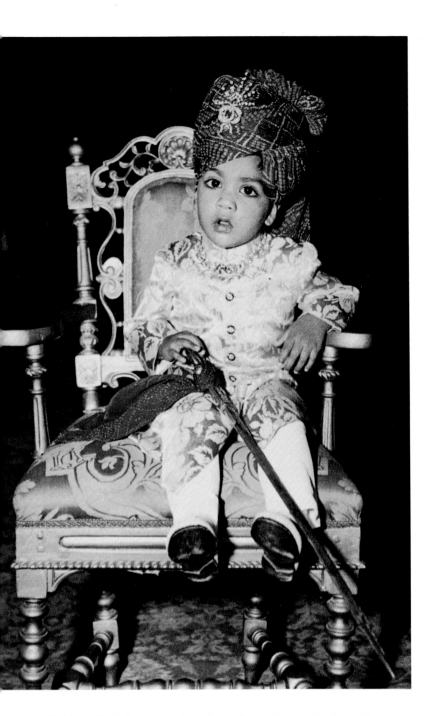

Childhood in India tends to be a charmed period, especially for a Prince or a Princess. British nannydom mixes with Indian sensuousness in the mechanically driven cradle on the facing page belonging to the father of the present Maharaja of Jodhpur. Angels are pushing it – but angels in saris, with bangles on their arms and *tilak* marks on their foreheads. The Maharaja is shown (*above*) aged three and (*right*) aged four after acceding to the *gadi* of Jodhpur following his father's early death. He is also seen (*opposite*) aged ten, a few years before he was sent to Eton.

Rani Usha Devi, the wife of Maharaj Swarup Singh,
with her youngest son, Suryaveer Singh.

The daughter of the Maharaja and Maharani of Jodhpur is known as Baiji Lal (Princess) Shivranjani. She was born in 1974. Here she holds her pet dog Gimlet.

The widowed Rajmata of Jaiselmer, the mother of the Maharawal, is seen (*right*) against one of the pierced marble screens that are a fascinating feature of Jaiselmer's palaces and mansions (*havelis*).

Religion and politics are interwoven in India to an extent that has almost been forgotten in the West. The Maharaja of Jodhpur is a Hindu, and although he has been educated largely in the West, he still obeys certain Hindu traditions. His visits to the family shrine with the Maharani are naturally occasions of significance for the local people, who garland him and take his blessings.

Overleaf The cenotaphs of the rulers of Jodhpur, at Mandore outside the
modern city, were customarily erected on the spot where the Ranis burnt
themselves to death: the ritual immolation of a Hindu wife on her husband's
funeral pyre, known as *sati*. They are eerie, jumbled places, 'more quiet and
empty and lonely than any place on earth'.

3
BY ELEPHANT, HORSE OR ROLLS ROYCE
THE MAHARAJAS AT PLAY

The octagonal *gadi* (throne) in the
Pearl Palace of the Meherangarh, the
Fort of Jodhpur, is one of several
belonging to the long line of rulers of
the Rathore clan.

Important guests at the Laxmi Vilas Palace in Baroda fifty years ago used to be requested to tick an embossed card specifying the means of transport they would be requiring the following morning for the day's activities: was it to be Elephant, Horse, or Rolls Royce?

At Jodhpur one might have added 'Aeroplane' to the list. Maharaja Umaid Singh was one of India's early pilots. He opened not only an airport in his desert state but a Flying Club too. A British official, Sir John Steel, came from New Delhi to open it and the Maharaja's cameraman recorded the occasion. The Maharaja looks like an over-enthusiastic figure out of P. G. Wodehouse, while Sir John looks suitably steely beneath his *sola topee* (pith helmet). At the appropriate signal a key is produced, Sir John unlocks the hangar doors and a plane appears. Then there are loop-the-loops. We see the Maharaja's guests sitting on upholstered chairs arranged on a carpet in an enclosure, while their expensive, spotless motor-cars stand at the edge of the desert. 'Something in the atmosphere of this sequence,' says James Ivory in his inimitable series of vignettes of Princely life in those charmed decades between the wars, 'sums up that entire world. It all seems contained in one shot, across which a low sun is slanting: the desert, starting at the carpet's edge, stretches away into the distance; the little planes tumble about in the afternoon sky like gnats; the well-dressed people sit comfortably on their sofas, looking up; the shiny cars are standing ready with drivers and cleaners.'

Not all Maharajas could boast an aeroplane, but all of them had big motor-cars, and some had more than a hundred of the best makes. The Maharaja of Cooch Behar and the sixth Nizam of Hyderabad seem to have been first behind the wheel, in the 1890s. The first Rolls Royce (out of the eight hundred or so that made their way out east to India's Princes over the next forty years) belonged to the Maharaja of Gwalior; acquired in 1908, it was known as the 'Pearl of the East'. But it was Maharaja Bhupinder Singh of Patiala who had the biggest stable of Rolls's — some twenty-seven models as well as a hundred other cars. His fellow-Prince at Bharatpur had a taste for them as well; he once bought up a London showroom full of Rolls's, along with the services of an assistant whom he considered to be insolent. This unfortunate paraded the cars proudly before their owner at Bharatpur and received the shock of his career when the Maharaja ordered them to be taken away and used to cart municipal rubbish.

In Hyderabad the seventh Nizam developed a penchant for collecting limousines. These often belonged to other people; the Nizam would ask their owners if he might take a ride and then order his chauffeur to drive the car in question to the palace garage. By fair means and foul, he collected more than two hundred luxury vehicles and simply stored them away virtually unused.

The pace of Princely purchase of fine automobiles came more or less to a halt during the Second World War, for obvious reasons, and never revived. Nevertheless, the hedonistic Maharaja Pratap Sinha of Baroda, the grandson of Sayaji Rao, was able to lay claim to the first Rolls out of the factory after the war.

It wasn't all Rolls's among the Princes either. The dubious but captivating Maharaja of Alwar had a fleet of Hispano-Suizas, finished in blue and purchased in threes. He also had a Lanchester custom-built in England in 1924, which was golden inside and out. Its driver and his companion sat in the open on gold cushions. The back portion was a facsimile of the British coronation coach, complete with carriage lamps and gold crowns. Right at the back, instead of a dicky- or rumble-seat proper there was a seat for two footmen. The steering-wheel was made of ivory and, because the Maharaja had a fetish against leather of any kind, the upholstery, and even parts of the suspension where necessary, were made of other materials. The car was capable of rolling precisely at three miles an hour in line with a procession of the Alwar Lancers, or of cruising at eighty if required.

The Maharaja's final journey took place in this outlandish vehicle. He died of apoplexy in Paris in 1937. The car met his body at the border of the State, as the ruler had directed. With the Maharaja seated upright, impeccably dressed down to the white gloves he habitually wore in life, and wearing dark glasses to protect his sightless eyes from the rays of the summer sun in Rajasthan, the 'golden hearse' (in John Lord's phrase) made its stately way to the burning ground; and it is said that, despite his justified reputation as a sadist, people wept for their ruler. The scene would beggar even the baroque imagination of Federico Fellini.

Lastly, there was the collection of Maharaja Jagatjit Singh of Kapurthala, a Francophile who had built, in the grounds of his palace, a large circular structure known as the *Elysées Curées*. Its outer ring was a stables for the palace, its inner a motor garage. 'My sister and I used to cycle over there with carrots and go round feeding all the horses,' recalls the grandson of Jagatjit Singh. After that they would take a look at all the cars lined up. 'Whenever I get a whiff of that genuine smell of leather it takes me back to my grandfather's Hispano-Suiza, a lovely old thing which had a telephone in the back seat. You pressed a button and spoke into the telephone and told the driver where to go.' There was also a more modern Buick with two jump seats 'beautifully lined in velvet that fell out from the front seat's back-rest.'

While cars were largely ornamental to the princes, horses were a serious matter. In *From Sea to Sea* Kipling gives a detailed description of the Jodhpur stables and stud in 1887 which left even him reeling, since he reckoned that the Maharaja owned nearer twelve hundred horses than a thousand, of just about every breed. The Maharaja gave them names like *Raja*,

Autocrat, Turquoise, Eclipse, Young Revenge and *Sherwood*, and won many prizes with them. Rather than any horse being shot at the end of its useful life, it would be allowed to die of natural causes, be wrapped in a white sheet strewn with flowers and, 'amid the weeping of syces', be borne away to the burial ground in the desert. Kipling quickly became convinced that 'All Jodhpur is horse-mad . . . and it behoves any one who wishes to be any one to keep his own race-course.'

Young Princes were trained to ride, and thereafter to stick pig and play polo, from as tender an age as three years old. Karan Singh of Kashmir, for instance, whose father Hari Singh loved polo and was fanatical about racing, was forced to ride every day of his life, 'beginning on a box saddle and a tiny horse and gradually moving on to larger animals'. He had several falls, and was once terrified when his horse bolted on the polo ground at Jammu; he managed to hang onto it until it finally exhausted itself and came to a halt.

Later in his life, during his late teens, when the family moved to Bombay after Independence, his father indulged his passion for racing to the full, seldom fielding less than two horses every week, often four. 'There were gallops and spurts, small race books and large ones, confabulations with jockeys and trainers, thinly veiled animosity towards rival owners and, finally, race day on Saturday or Sunday. It seemed as if the whole week was a preparation for this event. . . .

Quite clearly, my father was much happier racing than administering the State.'

The horse was also a vital part of certain kinds of hunting, in particular that of the beautiful black buck. In Rajput miniatures this animal is often shown dashing away from a Raja (and sometimes his Ranis) who are in hot pursuit on horseback, its spiralling horns and black and white mask giving it a dramatic, masculine grace. This last attribute means that it is also often seen in paintings, being caressed as a symbol of a maiden's absent love; while in poetry, it becomes her four-footed confidant.

From about the turn of this century Princely hunts became a much more developed affair than before, geared to the visits of the British Viceroys, Governors and other officials, and even two Princes of Wales (in 1905 and 1922) determined to bag some tigers and other game. To make their guests' sojourn in the jungle agreeable, the Princes laid on carpeted tents, Fortnum and Mason delicacies, supplies of champagne and so on. Elephants were the preferred mode of transport, but if the terrain permitted it, a shooting brake (which in Bharatpur was a converted Rolls Royce) would be used.

The Maharaja of Gwalior was one of the most dedicated tiger hunters. By 1965 he had bagged 1400 of them. The Maharaja of Cooch Behar, a jungle state, shot 365 tigers, 438 buffaloes, 207 rhinoceroses and 311 leopards. Even his sister, the slight-seeming Gayatri

Devi, bagged 27 tigers before she turned conservationist.

Lady Birdwood, the daughter of a famous British political officer Sir George Ogilvie, who spent many weeks in the jungle accompanying shikar parties, comments today with more than a touch of disgust that 'they shot everything which moved or flew'. This seems to be quite literally true of the best-known bird shoot in India, at Gajner Lake, a patch of water about four or five acres in extent in the desert, twenty miles from Bikaner. Every September/October thousands of Imperial Sand Grouse would descend on the lake in an extraordinary migration from Arctic regions. When the Prince of Wales shot there in 1905, something like a hundred thousand grouse were on the lake. Nowadays, only about five thousand come, because the irrigation systems have drawn them away.

The whole idea and organization of this shoot was the brainchild of the formidable Maharaja Ganga Singh of Bikaner, who derived considerable benefit from it in other ways; in the gaps between firing he was able to conduct some informal business with the Viceroys and their officials. They were always given the best-sited butts, of course, and a decent bag was always ensured for them regardless of the accuracy of their shooting. Such precautions were unnecessary in the case of Lord Linlithgow, who was a fine shot and used to visit Gajner at least twice a year (in defiance of the protocol that a State should be visited not more than once annually), or Lord Mountbatten, who bagged fifty brace of grouse in a morning. Though the grouse were hard to hit, a typical morning's bag would be around four thousand birds.

A local folksong looks at life from a grouse's eye view, rather than a Viceroy's. The grouse (or *talor*) visit the lake in the early morning and at sunset, sheltering during the day among the bare rocks where they blend into the background:

> Her white and yellow flecked wings
> merge with the grass.
> She sits still as a dried-up cow-pat
> as Holwa the hawk circles overhead.

It is no exaggeration to say that such songs, and hundreds like them, are a potent force in keeping the Rajput peasants alive in their unforgiving desert land. 'It was the music that led me to try and discover the people,' says Uma Amand; 'a music that invades the spaces of the wasteland, reverberates against the upturned cauldron of a brazen sky, to invest each barren hamlet with the bounty of living.'

Ballads have been the most powerful way of preserving Rajput values over the centuries, and a unifying bond between the Prince and his subjects. The Ballad of Pabuji is especially famous, combining history, myth and legend. It concerns the illegitimate son of a Rathore

Prince, who is known to have lived. He fell in love with a fairy. She lived with him at night but extracted a promise from him that he would not intrude upon her during the day. She bore him a son. The Prince did not keep his promise, but on entering her apartments he came upon a lioness feeding the baby. The lioness vanished on catching sight of the Prince. But her sister Devali, a sturdy woman with mystical powers, brought the boy up. His pranks as a child and his exploits as a young man, rather like those in the ubiquitous Krishna legend, are the stuff of the ballad. His birthplace is said to be at Kolu near Pokharan, between Jodhpur and Jaiselmer. A well still exists there, said to have been dug by the boy Pabu and his companions. He is also a pastoral hero, credited with introducing a new breed of camel into the region, and the patron deity of a certain community who are camel drovers and herdsmen.

The Rajput rulers patronized these balladeers and musicians while living in their desert encampments and in their palaces. Every major state, and many minor ones, had its *gharana* or music school which gave its name to the style of playing or singing that developed there. Thus Ustad Allauddin Khan, the greatest instrumentalist India has known in modern times (the father of Ustad Ali Akbar Khan and father-in-law of Ravi Shankar), belonged to the *gharana* of the Nawab of Rampur, though he later became the court composer at a small central Indian state, Maihar.

At Jaiselmer, where the Maharawal was also a great patron of music, the palace musicians would play four times a day, with ragas on the *shehnai* (a penetrating reed instrument used for weddings and funerals which somewhat resembles the bag pipe) accompanied by *nagara* (drums) and the *sarengi* (a piercing violin-like instrument). The ruler Jawahir Singhji would stand and say 'Wah, wah!' – the appreciative sound made by a connoisseur of Indian classical music – to encourage them.

Perhaps because of its extreme isolation among the sands of the Thar Desert, Jaiselmer has developed a particularly strong musical tradition, the keepers of which are known as *manganiyars*, which means 'ones who beg'. 'Not only was it the duty of the *manganiyar* to entertain the Rajput before and after battle,' says Uma Anand, 'but it was also customary for the chief *manganiyar* to stay by the ruler when he died, to accompany his cortege to the cremation ground, and to remain there day and night, in constant vigil, till the ceremonies for the peace of the departed soul were concluded, and the period of mourning was over.'

With Princely rule gone, the *manganiyars* no longer have a role. In 1973 the son of the last great troubadour of the Jaiselmer court, Akbar Shah, was working in a government office as a messenger when, prompted by a certain request, he sent word around the villages near Jaiselmer for the *manganiyars* to assemble at a field camp.

They were to be recorded, in exchange for cash to help them get through the fifth successive year of drought in the region. They also recognized the opportunity to build a new audience for their music, as has subsequently happened through radio performances in India, an annual desert festival, and the attention of foreign film teams.

On this occasion, the *manganiyars* played and sang intensively over several days. Uma Anand was present throughout and regards it as the most exciting traditional music she has ever heard in India. She was totally overwhelmed. 'Late into that last night the *manganiyars* continued to sing and play with no hint of fatigue, or flagging of voices. I walked out into the cold dark courtyard, under an open sky ablaze and crackling with stars, listening in wonder to the sound of their music which seemed to well out of the earth under my feet. I asked myself: from what secret reserve do they draw such strength? . . . What hidden springs nourish the unquenchable flow of their music which gushes out, to make what is barren, green with beauty?'

She and her companions left the field camp at three in the morning. It was strangely quiet. As they walked to their car they were taken aback to find the *manganiyars* lined up in two silent rows on either side of the path to the gate, in the biting pre-dawn cold. 'We moved slowly past this guard of honour which solemnly greeted us with that ceremonial *namaste* which is traditionally reserved for royalty. We were so moved we could barely respond. I hurried into the vehicle and stared, unseeing, at the blurred landscape.'

Another tradition of the region of equal longevity to that of the *manganiyars* is *kathputli*, or puppeteering, using dolls of about 12 to 18 inches in height with wooden heads and bodies of stuffed cloth with arms but no legs. It is better known than Jaiselmer's folk music, at least partly because the puppeteers have travelled all over India through the centuries and were seen and described by British writers in the early part of the last century (who had mixed feelings about them).

Today, there are usually no more than a dozen dolls in a puppeteer's collection, for reasons of expense, and because the doll-carving skills are dying out. A full set consists of thirty-two characters, from Princes and Princesses to heroes, clowns, stock characters like the quarrelsome washerman and his wife (a Rajput Punch and Judy), and animals and reptiles.

The story with the hoariest tradition performed by these puppeteers concerns a real Prince of Jodhpur, Amar Singh, the son of Maharaja Gaj Singh who ruled Jodhpur from 1620 to 1638 at the time of the Moghul Emperor Shah Jehan. A valiant warrior, he was heir to the *gadi* of Jodhpur, but he threw away his chances through his rash temperament. His younger brother, Jaswant Singh, was both a great fighter and a diplomat. He obtained the *gadi* by ingratiating himself with his

95

father's favourite mistress. (A pair of slippers now in the Fort Museum at Jodhpur is said to have been slipped onto her feet by Jaswant Singh.) Amar Singh was exiled from Jodhpur and took himself off to the Moghul court at Agra in disgust.

There he spoilt his chances for good by the same uncontrollable temper. In the Diwan-i-Khas (Hall of Private Audience) at Agra Fort he slew Shah Jehan's paymaster, Salabat Khan, and attempted to strike the Emperor himself, but his sword struck a pillar and shattered. Maddened by opium, he ran amok and slaughtered five Moghul noblemen with his dagger before dying at the hand of his brother-in-law Arjun Singh Gaur of Bundi. His wife, a Bundi Princess, came to Agra and became *sati* on his funeral pyre. A mark on a pillar in the Diwan-i-Khas today is said to be the spot where Amar Singh's weapon struck, and the south gate of the Fort bears his name – a remarkable tribute to his personality, considering his behaviour.

In his own lifetime he became both a hero and a legend in Rajasthan. 'His death at the imperial court only enhanced his prestige in the eyes of the common folk,' comments Uma Anand, 'who celebrated him' – as they do today – 'as a martyr to Rajput honour.'

This palanquin was captured in a war with Gujerat in 1730 by Raja Abhaisinghji of Jodhpur. It has six carrying handles and its outside surface consists mainly of delicate filigree work, which allowed its royal occupants to breathe a little more easily behind the overhanging curtains that once covered it.

Rajput weddings were formerly occasions of astonishing opulence lasting several weeks because of the distances and difficulties involved in getting to them. Nowadays, a bridegroom can pick his transport according to taste: elephant (Udaipur), horse (Jodhpur), or vintage motor-car (Jaiselmer).

The Maharajas adored smart cars and motoring; stories are legion of the number they acquired (especially Rolls Royces), and the extraordinary uses to which they were put. Relatively few remain. Various members of the Jodhpur royal family can be seen in an MG (*above*). One of them, Raghvender Singh, takes the wheel in *Brideshead*-mood (*bottom left*); while the Maharaja of Kishengarh (*top left*) stands beside something a little more sedate.

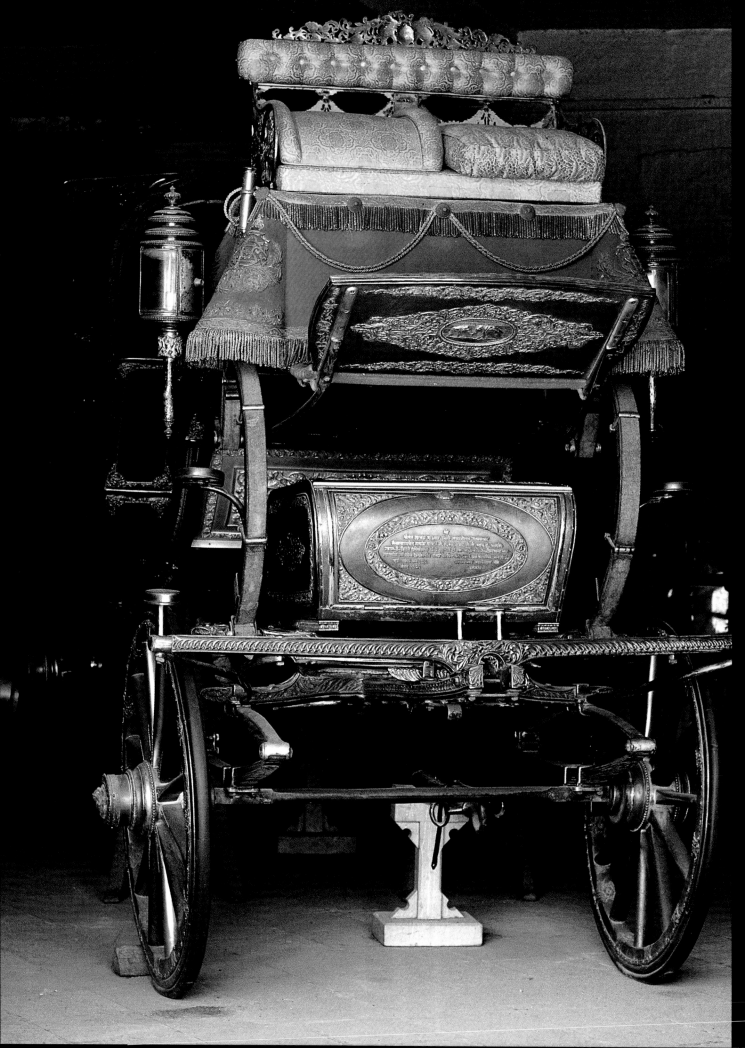

Not all the Maharajas felt the need to
import a coach. One of these (*left*)
belongs to the Maharaja of
Dhrangadhara, whose son the Maharaj
Kumar Yuvaraj Singh sits grandly in it,
the other (*far left*) to Lt. Col.
Fatesinghrao, the Gaekwad of Baroda,
who married his late wife in it. She was a
Jodhpur princess who flew solo at the age
of thirteen.

Maharajas are more often pictured on elephants than horses. In fact, many of them were superb riders, trained from the age of only three or four – a habit encouraged by the British during the Raj. They relished pig-sticking from horseback every bit much as British army officers, and some of them excelled at polo, especially the late Maharaja Jai Singh of Jaipur, a friend of many British aristocrats, who died on the polo field in England at Cirencester in 1970. The present Maharaja of Jodhpur (*right*) is no exception to an ancestral tradition of horsemanship.

The miniature painting shows a game of polo in progress at Jodhpur. The present Maharaja of Jodhpur takes a rather more leisurely canter around a field near his palace. The horse's inward-pointing ears are typical of the Jodhpur breed. Kipling, in 1887, estimated that the Maharaja had about 1200 horses.

The royal hunt of the Jodhpurs, depicted in a miniature painting; perhaps surprisingly, the Raja is accompanied by his Ranis. In the first half of the twentieth century, the Maharajas (and their British guests) slaughtered game on an unprecedented scale. The Maharaja of Jodhpur (*top right*) still shoots, but others, including Dr Karni Singh, the Maharaja of Bikaner (*bottom right*), an Olympic clay-pigeon shot, have become conservationists.

The music of Rajasthan seems as timeless and as haunting as the desert itself, as Satyajit Ray has proved in two films set there. Here, local musicians play *sarengi* (*below*) and flute (*bottom*). An exotic import, a Western-style band (*right*), celebrates the Maharaja of Jodhpur's birthday according to the Western calendar.

At the time of *Diwali*, the nationwide Festival of Lights in October or November, dancers perform outdoors for the royal family of Jodhpur in the Meherangarh (the Fort).

The dancers perform in a folk style belonging to Rajasthan, known as *ghoomar*, involving at least two women and the telling of a legendary story. There are many graceful movements of the feet and body, but no language of hand-gestures, unlike classical Hindu dance forms such as *Bharata Natyam*.

Village women at a desert festival near Jaiselmer dance *ghoomar*, but in rather more rustic manner than in the fort at Jodhpur.

Overleaf Puppets, known as *kathputli*, have a long-standing tradition in Rajasthan. These are at Jaiselmer. They are operated by strings held by hands above their heads. The stories depicted are taken from martial legends of the Rajputs (especially the hot-tempered life and death of Amar Singh of Jodhpur), and from everyday life – the eternal bickering of the *dhobi-dhoban* (the washerman and his wife) is a favourite. The brown faces traditionally represent evil characters.

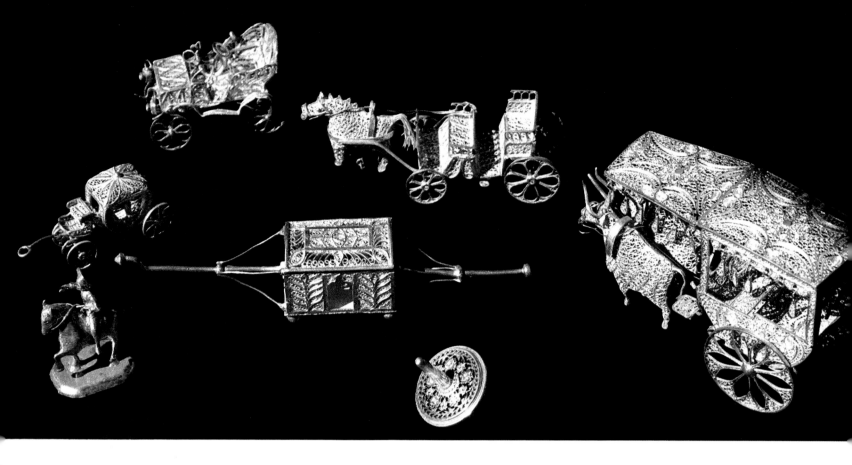

4
DIWAN-I-KHAS AND DIWAN-I-AM
THE FORTRESSES AND PALACES
OF THE MAHARAJAS

Silver toys in the collection of the
Maharaja of Dhrangadhara include
most forms of available transport, bar
the elephant. Chess has been played in
India since ancient times: this set
belongs to the Maharaja of Jodhpur.

No one who has seen the palaces of the Rajputs has been left unmarked by the experience. Little wonder that the pioneer art historian E. B. Havell wrote of them in 1890:

If our poets had sung them,
our painters had pictured them,
our heros and famous men had lived in them,
their romantic beauty would be on everyman's
    lips in Europe.

Yet a greater contrast in palaces could hardly be imagined than the two belonging to the ruling family of Jodhpur. Up on its rock the Meherangarh, the Fort of Jodhpur, built from 1459, is very forbidding indeed; inside, it is a succession of palaces within palaces of insane complexity, a maze of intricate marble screens and the faintly sinister overhanging eaves typical of much Rajput architecture, which are also found on the cenotaphs of the rulers at Mandore. Several hundred feet below spreads the city, and above it, on another escarpment lower than the Fort, stands something resembling a Victorian town hall, the Umaid Bhavan, begun by Maharaja Umaid Singh in 1929, the last great palace to be built in India, a 'white elephant' (in the Gaekwad of Baroda's amusing phrase) from its conception, and now a hotel.

Even if one excludes the ancient fortresses of the Princes, at Gwalior, Chitor, Amber, Bharatpur, Jodh-pur, Bikaner and Jaiselmer, among others, and considers only the palaces built not primarily for defence, there is no cohesion of style. It is impossible to compare the Rajput-Moghul fusions of the highly planned city of Jaipur (begun in 1728) with the eclectic muddle of Laxmi Vilas at Baroda (completed in 1890), the baroque clutter of the Falaknuma palace at Hyderabad (built in 1872) and the stolidity of the Umaid Bhavan at Jodhpur. It may fairly be said that the palaces built in the heyday of the Maharajas from the 1860s up to the 1930s, with their flamboyant gamut of styles, matched the eccentricites of their patrons. They are 'facilities for dedicated jollifica-tion', according to the Gaekwad, who should know; 'to the architectural purist such buildings can only be regarded as gorgeous trash.'

Nevertheless, among their bizarre profusion of styles, two trends are discernible: first, a blend of Indian and Islamic styles, which went under the general name 'Indo-Saracenic' and conveyed an air of Moorishness; secondly, an attempt to adapt European styles to Indian conditions, dubbed 'Renaissance Oriental' by the Gaekwad. His own family's palace is a good example of the former trend, while the Umaid Bhavan and the buildings of Lutyens' New Delhi epitomize the latter.

The palace at Baroda is so enormous that it took the present Maharaja (the Gaekwad) a year or two to find his way round it as a child; today he admits there are parts he has not visited for the last fifteen years or more. Its construction came about because Sayaji Rao came to feel that the old Nazar Bagh Palace was dark, cavernous and better suited as a storehouse for the family jewels. Probably he also thought it had too many associations with the barbarities of his predecessors.

The replacement took twelve years to build, at a cost of around £180,000. Its architect, like that of so many Princely extravaganzas, was a British army officer with a taste for experiment and a sympathy with the country: in this case, Major Charles Mant of the Royal Engineers. He had arrived in India in 1859. One of his early buildings there was a town hall in the state of Kolhapur in an Italian Gothic style, but he soon became fascinated by native Indian architecture, and an exponent of the 'Indo-Saracenic' style, which he employed at Florence in 1870 for a monument to the young heir of Kolhapur who had died there. Later, he produced designs for palaces at Cooch Behar, Darbhanga, Kolhapur and Baroda. He lived to see the completion of none of them though, because he lost his mind, persuaded that all his designs would collapse when built due to his faulty calculations, and died while still in his forties.

His design at Baroda was executed by Robert Fellowes Chisholm, following Mant's notion of preserving the traditional division of a ruler's palace into the rooms of Public Audience and of Private Audience, and the ladies' apartments (the Moghuls' Diwan-i-Am, Diwan-i-Khas and Zenana, respectively) while adding rooms and elements suitable to a more modern, Western way of living. Hence there came into being state banqueting rooms, billiard rooms and great apartments for distinguished European guests (which were no doubt fitted with European sanitary ware of the best kind too).

Mant allowed various styles to melt into one another, and he (and later Chisholm) was able to get away with this because of the very long frontage of the palace at Baroda – over five hundred feet in length. As its present owner observes, 'The exterior of the Maharaja's apartments was dressed up in the garb of Hindu martial architecture, with most of the detail borrowed from the fortress of Bharatpur. The public apartments, however, moved more into a Moghul style, while the ladies' quarters ended in a forest of domes and canopies copied from the Jain temples of Gujerat.'

The materials used to build these structures were Indian, but the trimmings were distinctly European, following the taste of most later Maharajas for buying up large quantities of the best of anything available in the fanciest department stores of the capitals of Europe. In Sayaji Rao's case, the craftsmen came too. The Durbar Hall has a Venetian mosaic floor which took twelve Venetian workmen eighteen months to lay. The doorways, pillars and ornamental staircase in this hall are made from Carrara marble. The moulding and gilding on the walls and ceilings was done by a Mr Tree from

London, while the gardens were the handiwork of a Mr Goldring from Kew. The sculptures on the staircase were by Signor Felici from Italy, while Mr Dix from London created the stained-glass windows. The great chandeliers, without which no Maharaja's palace was complete, were Venetian. Thus the entirety could be seen as Baroda's version of the meeting of East and West.

The Umaid Bhavan in Jodhpur, which the Gaekwad of Baroda nicely terms 'civic-monolithic' in style, is a work of altogether less distinction. Its architect, H. V. Lanchester, whose career included town halls at Cardiff and Deptford, a university at Leeds and hospitals in London and Birmingham, did not share Major Mant's Indian imaginings. 'In the architectural treatment and ornamental detail, any use of "Indo-Saracenic" features was regarded as inappropriate in view of the fact that the States of Rajasthan only came to a very limited extent under Muslim domination,' he asserted. Why that should have made a wholly English style more appropriate, Lanchester did not explain. One senses that he was, in Forsterian terms, a Ronnie Heaslop to Major Mant's Fielding.

Inside, the palace is definitely a hybrid of the wildest kind. It has 347 rooms, including 8 dining rooms and a banqueting hall for 300 people. Its dome rises to a height of 190 feet; in its bowels is a swimming pool with foamy 1930s murals. There were suites for Princes and Princesses, and suites for commoners, and in the grandest of these, the Oriental Room, a Polish artist, S. Norblin, was called in to paint modern interpretations of the great Hindu epic the Mahabharata, of hideous incongruity. Yet what could be more incongruous than the whole notion of the palace itself, like a huge passenger liner, 'becalmed in a dead sea of sand and hot rock', in the words of Ivory, who stayed there several times when dreaming about his films of Princely India?

Probably its most foolish aspect was its siting, chosen for astrological reasons on a hill, thus creating tremendous problems with the water supply, and the need for endless donkeys to carry the earth for the palace base to the top of the hill, plus twelve miles of railway track to transport the required cream-pink sandstone from the nearest quarry.

But Umaid Singh must really have welcomed the extra work thus generated, because he had ordered the palace in the first place as a boon to his people, who were starving from lack of monsoon rains for the third year in succession. Only a Maharaja could have conceived of such a supremely useless programme of public works. Twenty miles from Jodhpur, at Sada Samand, on the edge of trackless desert, he completed his folly, with a small retreat. It has a bar, with leopard-skin-clad high stools and an indescribably awful elephant-foot bar-lamp, which reminded Ivory of the bars on old transcontinental trains in the USA. But 'it would have taken many drinks to make this seem as nice a place. . . .

At Sada Samand I felt as if I had arrived at the farthest edge of civilisation. Below those ramparts there was nothing, a soundless void.'

The minor palaces sometimes offer a perfection of scale and decoration not available in their more grandiose counterparts. The palace at Samod, north of Jaipur, was built around the time that Jaipur was established (from 1728); in fact the Raval of Samod appears to have been inspired by the work there.

Its finest features are its wall-paintings and its mirror-work, in the Sheesh Mahal (Mirror Palace). As Uma Anand points out, these rooms are best viewed as they were meant to be seen, seated on a very low divan, reclining against a bolster. Then, as the eye travels upwards, one sees first paintings of everyday incidents – Princes and Princesses hunting deer, girls on a swing or lovers in a bower. Above them come panels of formal design, floral or geometric. Then, leaning back, one takes in scenes of court life – durbars, processions and triumphant victory parades – and finally, the glittering stars in the ceiling. In the finest Sheesh Mahal of all, built in 1639 at Amber by Jai Singh I, 'when the doors are closed,' says Uma Anand, 'in the light of a single candle, one loses all sense of confinement, and floats like a satellite in infinite space among the glittering galaxies.'

The Rajput rulers who ordered this mirrorwork (which has its origin in Persia) knew nothing about satellites, of course, but everything about the majesty of the star-studded night sky in the desert, as they took their leisure accompanied by the haunting ragas of the *manganiyars*, their court musicians. The Sheesh Mahals, which were essentially public chambers used for celebrations of births, marriages and victories, were designed to remind the rulers of the night sky that was their usual canopy. The editor of the 1920 edition of Tod's *Annals* notes that a whole industry of blowing glass globes, silvered inside, grew up to meet the demand for Sheesh Mahals. The globes were then broken into fragments and set in cement (or in Burma in lacquer).

Such palaces, and indeed all those built in India before the last century, would have contained very little furniture, partly in recognition of the need to let whatever breeze there might be blow freely, and partly as a matter of taste. Until the cluttered British drawing rooms of Delhi and Calcutta began to be widely copied, the contents of a palace were mainly wallhangings, murals and carpets. 'There might be a few silver and gold ivory beds', observes Gayatri Devi, 'and perhaps some richly carved chests, but for the most part low wooden platforms, mattresses, and bolsters provided the sitting accommodation.'

This is certainly largely true, even today, of the City Palace at Udaipur, and it would formerly have been true too (before it became a hotel) of its sister palace, the Jagnivas, in the middle of the Pichola Lake, where – as a contemporary chronicler put it – the Rajput nobles would once upon a time recline and

listen to the tales of the bard, and sleep off their noonday opiate amidst the cool breezes of the lake, wafting delicious odours from the myriads of the lotus flower which covered the surface of the waters; and as the fumes of the potion evaporated, they [would open] their eyes on a landscape to which not even its inspiration could frame an equal. . . . Amid such scenes did the princes and chieftains recreate during two generations, exchanging the din of arms for voluptuous inactivity.

They had left behind them the grimness of their old fortress at Chitor, with its charred memories of mass death. But the first of the many palaces of Udaipur, the City Palace built by Udai Singh after he fled Chitor in 1567, very strongly recalls Chitor from the outside. Its walls are tremendously long, sheer and undecorated, rising straight out of the waters of the Lake, and most of the flourishes visible are safely at the top. Inside the palace, it is all flourish, recalling the court of the Moghuls who had subdued Chitor. Everything seems to be of marble except the proliferating inlay, painting and mosaics in geometric and florid patterns that decorate even the most improbable surfaces.

It is fitting that the Moghul Emperor Shah Jehan, who created the Taj Mahal – itself 'one solitary tear hanging on the cheek of time' (to quote Tagore) – should have whiled away four months in 1623 as a young man at Udaipur in a palace on the Pichola Lake. As Prince Khurram, he was escaping the displeasure of his father Jehangir who suspected him of plotting against his interests. He lived, not in the Lake Palace itself (which was not then in existence), but in the Gul Mahal, a just-completed domed pavilion in the Jagmandir in another part of the lake.

But, for all the breath-taking loveliness of the palaces on the Pichola Lake (which inspired Kipling to remark that 'If the Venetian owned [it] he might say. with justice: "See it and die"'), they are really fairy-tale diversions from the real world of Royal Rajputana, the fortresses. There can be none more evocative of this than the battlements of Jaiselmer, 'a huge fortification at the world's end' (according to the Gaekwad again) which seems to crouch like an ancient tawny lion in the desert sands. Satyajit Ray was so taken with it that he wrote a story about it for children in which a peacock guards an imaginary treasure hoard inside the fortress, and then made a film out of the story called *Sonar Kella* ('The Golden Fortress'). The name is no hyperbole; the limestone of the region is a pale yellow that has been burnished to a deep gold by wind and sand.

When Ray was there in 1968 (just after the railway reached Jaiselmer) to make an earlier film, his first in Rajasthan, he met the Maharawal, who showed him some interesting objects made out of the golden stone of the fortress: a tumbler, a teacup, a spoon, a necklace, some cuff links. 'The gleaming purity of the saffron Jaiselmer marble made us hold our breath. It was if gold had renounced its lustre and turned ascetic.'

'Bring a bowl of water,' ordered the Maharaja, and the bearer obliged by bringing a blue plastic bowl half filled with water. The tea cup and the tumbler were now gently placed in the water. They stayed on the surface, floating. It was like magic, and we all but applauded.

'They were made by a Muslim craftsman who is now dead. These were his last gifts to me. The only other craftsman who could carve them so thin and with such perfect balance has gone to Pakistan.'

The fortress itself dates from 1156 when Raja Jaisal, who was already chief of a neighbouring fort, discovered the Gadisar Lake and the three-peaked hill above it, which was then the home of a hermit. He, it is said, invited Jaisal to build a fort. The spot seemed an excellent one, with water available and secure defences. Jaisal and his descendants threw ninety-nine bastions around the hill and inside them built a city, with a series of palaces, Jain temples and merchants' houses (*havelis*) of quite astonishing intricacy.

The trade that made the city rich and the construction of all these buildings possible, was that of the caravan routes into India from the west. This lasted for seven centuries until the coming of the sea passage for goods with the opening of the Suez Canal in 1869. Jaiselmer, and its main market square Manik Chowk, groaned, in its time, with the dried fruits of Basra and Isphahan, nuts of all varieties including the pistachios from which the delicious sweet *piste-ki-laus* was made, carpets from Herat, furs from Kabul, swords and scimitars from Damascus, casks of perfumed wine from Shiraz, Arab stallions, slaves from Turkestan and Abyssinia and, in Uma Anand's words, 'those legendary, green-eyed Circassian houris abducted from unknown mountain kingdoms, who fetched fabulous prices and were the pride of the harems of Hindustan.'

It also boasts a history which, if not quite as blood-stained as that of Chitor, must be the longest catalogue of deceit in all Rajputana. This culminated in the early nineteenth century with the rise to influence of a merchant Prime Minister, Salim Singh, who appeared outwardly innocent, but inside seemed to cherish the most grasping and murderous intentions. He bound the ruler of the time hand and foot with spies and was in effective charge of the kingdom until his murder in 1824, stabbed by a desperate Rajput. As a disgusted Tod, who had just retired as Political Agent, notes: 'since there was some fear that the wound might heal, his wife gave him poison'!

Salim Singh's *haveli*, perched with its drooping eaves on top of a tower (presumably in a vain attempt to escape revenge), is one of the most interesting and refined structures in Jaiselmer today, a city to which Kipling, if he had made the long dusty journey in 1887, would surely have applied the language he used on the fort at Amber, but with knobs on. He was very disturbed by Amber's 'venomous and suggestive little rooms' which were 'crampt and darkened' and the 'narrow smooth-walled passages with recesses where a man might wait for his enemy unseen, the maze of ascending and descending stairs leading nowhither, the ever-present screens of marble tracery that may hide or reveal so much, – all these things breathe of plot and counter-plot, league and intrigue. In a living palace where the sightseer knows and feels that there are human beings everywhere, and that he is followed by scores of unseen eyes, the impression is almost unendurable.'

Notwithstanding the whiff of paranoia about native untrustworthiness mixed with the greatest sensitivity that is peculiarly Kipling's, his impression of a hundred years ago holds good today, and one suspects that many of the Princes of the time, who commissioned British architects to design their new palaces, like Umaid Singh of Jodhpur, may have been prey to comparable feelings about their bloody pasts. But they, like Kipling in Jodhpur, would have understood the uncomplicated clarity of the desert outside:

When the black dusk had shut down, the Englishman climbed up a little hill and saw stars come out and shine over the desert. Very far away, some camel drivers had lighted a fire and were singing as they sat by the side of their beasts. Sound travels as far over sand as over water, and their voices came into the city wall and beat against it in multiplied echoes.

On first inspection this courtyard with fountains looks as if it might be in Venice. It is in fact part of the Laxmi Vilas, the Gaekwad of Baroda's stupendous palace, finished in 1890. Twelve workmen from Venice spent eighteen months laying a floor of Venetian mosaic in the Durbar Hall.

Venetian chandeliers and Carrara marble in the massive entrance hall at Baroda complete the impression of Italy.

Overleaf The main entrance hall of the Umaid Bhavan Palace in Jodhpur hints at its strange origin. It was the last real palace to be built in India (not counting New Delhi); begun in 1929 by Maharaja Umaid Singh as a famine relief project, it took fifteen years to complete. The exterior has been called (by the Maharaja of Baroda) 'civic-monolithic', as befits the aim of its civic architect H. V. Lanchester. Inside is a 'confusion of Renaissance mimicry'.

More than a hundred years separate the painting of Maharaja Sardar Singh of Bikaner holding court, from the same view of the *gadi* (throne) today, and from the present Maharaja of Jodhpur and his son's court in the Phool Mahal (Flower Palace) of the Fort of Jodhpur. Today's ruler, though stripped of his power and title, has hardly less dignity; and the same is true of his courtiers.

Apart from the public areas of the Umaid Bhavan Palace there are 347 rooms, including eight dining rooms and a banqueting hall for 300 people. In the basement is a swimming pool with 1930s murals on its walls. The palace is now a hotel, and the Maharaja, seen above in what is now a foyer, lives in a wing of it with his family.

Raval Raghavendra Singh sits in his palace in Samod. The use of mirrors as an embellishment for walls and ceilings, seen here in the Sheesh Mahal (Mirror Palace) at Samod, is Persian in origin, but the Rajputs brought it to perfection. They reminded the rulers of the star-studded desert skies under which they spent most of their nights encamped.

The Takhat Vilas (*above*), in the Fort at Jodhpur, and used as a bedroom, reminds us how sparsely furnished Rajput palaces traditionally were. It took the influence of the nineteenth-century British to clutter them up with the more familiar trappings of European royalty.

The Flower Palace (*right*), also in the Fort, built by the Raja Abhai Singh in the early eighteenth century, is a fairytale structure with jewel-like stained-glass windows in golden filigree; gold-painted abstract designs on the ceiling and walls frame delicate miniatures.

The murals in the Oriental Room at
the Umaid Bhavan Palace were
painted in the 1940s by a Polish artist
invited by the Maharaja, despite the
fact that they depict stories from the
Indian epics. James Ivory calls them,
and the rest of the palace decor,
'Ashokan Art Deco'.

Overleaf The Umaid Bhavan Palace
overlooking the city of Jodhpur,
during the Festival of Lights –
celebrating the return from exile of
the famous lovers in the Ramayana
epic, Rama and Sita.

143

Overleaf The moonlit Jagnivas or Lake
Palace floats ethereally on the still
waters of the Pichola Lake.
Constructed by Maharana Jagat Singh
II of granite and white marble in the
mid eighteenth century, it is now a
famous hotel.

Probably the most romantic palaces in India are the two that face each other
across a lake at Udaipur, the City Palace and the Lake Palace. This peacock is
one of several which form a repeated motif inside the courtyards and rooms
of the City Palace. The cut-glass palace ornament overlooks the Pichola Lake
and gives a refracted hint of the sister palace which floats in its waters.

As a military stronghold, the Meherangarh, the Fort of Jodhpur, seen here from two angles, seems the most impregnable of all the fortresses in Rajasthan. It was built by Rao Jodha in 1459 and continuously added to inside, down to the last century. Kipling, seeing it in 1887, thought that only giants could have made it.

The fortress at Amber, in the hills above Jaipur, was the original home of the rulers of the area. It is a vast, sprawling complex of courtyards and fortifications, rumoured to contain untold treasure. Maharaja Jai Singh II moved out of it in 1728 to his planned city in the plain, the 'Pink City' of Jaipur, named after its pink sandstone and the matching pink paint used on its buildings.

SELECT BIBLIOGRAPHY

PLACE OF PUBLICATION IS LONDON UNLESS OTHERWISE STATED

Annals and Antiquities of Rajasthan by James Tod, Volumes 1–3 (First Edn., 1829–32. Second Edn., with an Introduction and Notes by William Crooke, 1920)

Autobiography of a Princess by James Ivory (1976)

Cartier – Jewelers Extraordinary by Hans Nadelhoffer (1984)

From Sea to Sea by Rudyard Kipling (New York, 1899)

The Great Moghuls by Bamber Gascoigne (1971)

Heir Apparent: An Autobiography by Karan Singh (New Delhi, 1982)

Highness: The Maharajahs of India by Ann Morrow (1986)

The Last Empire: Photography in British India, 1855–1911 by Clark Worswick and Ainsley Embree (New York, 1976)

Lives of the Indian Princes by Charles Allen and Sharada Dwivedi (1984)

The Maharajahs by John Lord (1972)

Mahatma by D. G. Tendulkar, Volumes 1–8 (Bombay, 1951–54)

The Making of the Indian Princes by Edward Thompson (1943)

Mansions of the Sun by Uma Anand (1982)

Our Films Their Films by Satyajit Ray (New Delhi, 1976)

The Palaces of India by The Maharaja of Baroda (1980)

Princely India by Clark Worswick (1980)

A Princess Remembers by Gayatri Devi and Santha Rama Rau (1976)

Rajasthan by Roloff Beny (1984)

Rajasthan: India's Enchanted Land by Raghubir Singh (1981)

The Rajput Palaces by G. H. R. Tillotson (1987)

Selected Poems – Rabindranath Tagore translated by William Radice (1985)

MAP: INDIA OF THE PRINCES

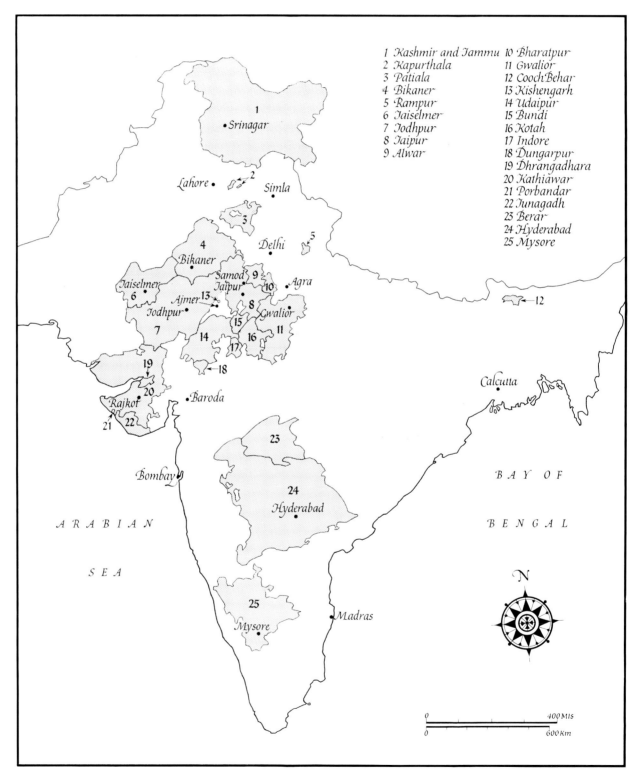

1 Kashmir and Jammu	10 Bharatpur
2 Kapurthala	11 Gwalior
3 Patiala	12 Cooch Behar
4 Bikaner	13 Kishengarh
5 Rampur	14 Udaipur
6 Jaiselmer	15 Bundi
7 Jodhpur	16 Kotah
8 Jaipur	17 Indore
9 Alwar	18 Dungarpur
	19 Dhrangadhara
	20 Kathiawar
	21 Porbandar
	22 Junagadh
	23 Berar
	24 Hyderabad
	25 Mysore

India of the Princes. The states shown are those mentioned in the text.

CHRONOLOGY OF EVENTS

c.	950 BC	Hindu epic poem Mahabharata written down
c.	750 BC	Hindu epic poem Ramayana written down
	AD 470	Rathor Rajputs found kingdom of Kanauj (traditional date)
c.	728	Bapu Rawal, chief of Sisodia Rajputs, founds kingdom of Mewar, after capturing Chitor
c.	928	Dhola Rae founds kingdom at Amber
	1156	Jaisal, chief of the Bhati Rajputs, founds Jaiselmer
	1211	Rathor Rajputs, driven from Kanauj, found kingdom of Marwar
	1303	First siege of Chitor by Alauddin Khilji, Pathan king of Delhi, first *johar* (holocaust) – 13,000 women burn themselves
	1459	City of Jodhpur founded by Raja Jodh of Marwar
	1488	City of Bikaner founded by Raja Bika from Marwar
	1527	Babur defeats Rajput confederacy and founds Moghul Empire
	1535	Second siege of Chitor by Sultan of Gujerat, second *johar*
	1556	Beginning of Akbar's reign as Moghul Emperor
	1565	Kingdom of Mysore established
	1567	Third siege of Chitor and sack by Akbar, third *johar*
		Rana Udai Singh founds new capital of Mewar at Udaipur
	1600	East India Company founded in Britain
	1605	Death of Akbar
	1620–38	Reign of Gaj Singh I at Jodhpur
	1623	Prince Khurram, later Emperor Shah Jehan, spends four months at Udaipur, after plotting against his father Jehangir
	1627	Accession of Shah Jehan
	1632–48	Taj Mahal built
	1658	Shah Jehan deposed by Aurangzeb
	1681	Bharatpur State founded
	1707	Death of Aurangzeb. Beginning of decline of Moghuls
	1724	Hyderabad State founded by Asaf Jah Nizam-ul-Mulk
	1728	Jaipur State and city founded by Raja Jai Singh II of Amber
	1732	Malhar Rao Holkar of Indore takes Malwa
	1739	Nadir Shah from Persia sacks Delhi
	1784	Madhaji Rao Scindia recaptures Gwalior Fort
	1799	British restore Mysore dynasty from rule of Tipu Sultan in Mysore
		Ranjit Singh establishes Sikh empire in Punjab
	1804	British conduct war against Holkar of Indore
	1817–18	British sign treaties with Maratha rulers and Rajput rulers
	1818–22	Tod Political Agent in Western Rajputana
	1824	Salim Singh, Prime Minister of Jaiselmer, poisoned
	1829–32	Publication of Tod's *Annals and Antiquities of Rajasthan*
	1845	First war between British and Sikhs
	1848	Second war between British and Sikhs, the Punjab annexed
	1857	Indian Mutiny
	1858	Government of India transferred from East India Company to the British Crown, Queen Victoria's proclamation concerning the Princes

1869	Birth of Mahatma Gandhi
1875	British depose Malhar Rao of Baroda and appoint Sayaji Rao
	Mayo College at Ajmer founded for sons of Princes
	Prince of Wales (later Edward VII) tours India
1876	Victoria proclaimed Queen-Empress of India
1877	First Durbar in Delhi
1878	Sayaji Rao begins building of Laxmi Vilas Palace in Baroda
1885	Indian National Congress founded
1887	Rudyard Kipling in Rajasthan
1889	Birth of Jawarharlal Nehru
1891	Dhuleep Singh dies
1901	Queen Victoria dies
1903	Second Delhi Durbar
1905	Lord Curzon retires as Viceroy
1911	Third Delhi Durbar with King George V present
	Sixth Nizam of Hyderabad and Berar dies
1914–18	First World War – Princes support British with troops
1916	Gandhi lambasts Princes at opening of Benares Hindu University
1918	Montagu-Chelmsford Report, beginning of reform of the system of government of India
1921	Chamber of Princes inaugurated
1922	Prince of Wales (later Edward VIII) tours India, Mountbatten in attendance
1929	Maharaja Umaid Singh of Jodhpur begins building Umaid Bhavan Palace
1930	Round Table Conference in London, attended by representatives of the Princes, the Muslim League and Liberals
1935	Government of India Act, dividing British India into eleven Provinces
1937	Deposed Maharaja of Alwar dies
1939–45	Second World War – Princes support Britain with troops
1942 (Aug.)	'Quit India' campaign led by Gandhi
1947 (Mar.)	Arrival of Lord Mountbatten as Viceroy
1947 (June)	Mountbatten announces date of Transfer of Power
1947 (July)	Mountbatten advises Chamber of Princes to sign Instruments of Accession to India or Pakistan
1947 (Aug.)	Independence of India and Pakistan, Maharaja of Kashmir flown to India
1947 (Oct.)	Invasion of Kashmir by Pakistani tribesmen
1947 (Dec.)	Eastern States merge with Indian Union, followed by other States
1948	'The most expensive wedding in the world' at Jaipur
1949	Nizam of Hyderabad and Berar accedes to Indian Union after a police action in Hyderabad
1952	First elections in Independent India – Maharaja Hanwant Singh of Jodhpur elected with a massive majority but dies in an air crash
	Karan Singh of Kashmir is installed as Sadar-i-Riyasat of Kashmir by Indian Government
1962	Gayatri Devi, Maharani of Jaipur, wins election as an opposition candidate with 175,000 vote majority – a world record
1967	Seventh Nizam of Hyderabad and Berar dies
1970	Maharaja Jai Singh of Jaipur dies, playing polo in Britain
1971	Indira Gandhi's government abolishes the Princely Order and their Privy Purses
1975–77	During Mrs Gandhi's Emergency various Princes and their families are put in jail, including Gayatri Devi of Jaipur
1987	A case of *sati* in a village near Jaipur leads to large pro-*sati* demonstrations in Jaipur

GUN SALUTES OF THE INDIAN PRINCES

Name of state	Area in square miles	Title of Ruler	Gun Salute
Baroda	8,164	Maharaja	21
Gwalior	26,382	Maharaja	21
Hyderabad	82,698	Nizam	21
Jammu and Kashmir	85,885	Maharaja	21
Mysore	29,528	Maharaja	21
Indore	9,519	Maharaja	19
Udaipur (Mewar)	12,915	Maharana	19
Bharatpur	1,982	Maharaja	17
Bikaner	23,315	Maharaja	17
Bundi	2,200	Maharao Raja	17
Jaipur	16,682	Maharaja	17
Jodhpur (Marwar)	35,066	Maharaja	17
Kotah	5,684	Maharaja	17
Patiala	5,932	Maharaja	17
Alwar	3,213	Maharaja	15
Dungarpur	1,447	Maharawal	15
Jaiselmer	16,062	Maharawal	15
Kishengarh	858	Maharaja	15
Rampur	893	Nawab	15
Bhavnagar	2,860	Maharaja	13
Cooch Behar	1,318	Maharaja	13
Dhrangadhara	1,157	Maharaja Raj Sahib	13
Junagadh	3,337	Nawab	13
Kapurthala	630	Maharaja	13
Nawanagar	3,791	Jam Saheb	13
Porbandar	642	Maharaja Rana Sahib	13
Ratlam	693	Maharaja	13
Dhrol	283	Thakor Sahib	9
Maihar	407	Raja	9
Rajkot	282	Thakor Sahib	9

ACKNOWLEDGMENTS

I would like to express my sincere gratitude to the Royal Family of Jodhpur for their support and assistance in the preparation of this book.

I would like to acknowledge and thank the following people:

> *H. H. Maharaja of Jodhpur Gaj Singh II;*
> *H. H. Maharaja of Baroda Fatesinghrao Gaekwad;*
> *H. H. Maharaja of Jaipur Sawai Bhawani Singh;*
> *H. H. Maharaja of Bikaner Karni Singh;*
> *H. H. Maharaja of Kishengarh Braji Raji Singh;*
> *Maharaj Kumar of Dhrangadhara Yuvaraj Singh;*
> *Raja of Poonch Ramon Deo Singh; Maharaj Swarup Singh;*
> *Maharaj Sobag Singh; Maharaj Prahard Singh;*
> *Maharaj Dalip Singh; Th. Raju Singh; Th. Sunder Singh;*
> *Th. Nah Singh/ Meherangarh Fort Museum; Mayo College;*
> *Miss Fumiko Shioda.*

And I would also like to express my appreciation to all the other people – too numerous to mention individually here – who assisted me during my photo sessions.

Sumio Uchiyama

INDEX

PAGE NUMBERS IN ITALIC REFER TO THE CAPTIONS TO THE PLATES